*W*ALKING
for Fitness & Health

WALKING
for Fitness & Health

Dr. Klaus Bos

Sterling Publishing Co., Inc.
New York

This book was written for people who want to maintain and improve their health and fitness through walking. The choice of walking program depends on age, fitness, and the health of the walker. Each reader must take personal responsibility for deciding whether and to what extent the exercises recommended by the author are appropriate. If you are not sure, you should seek medical advice.

Please pay attention to the notes in the text that warn you to get a physical examination or treatment before proceeding. In particular, read the discussions on pages 20–21 and take the Risk-Assessment Test before walking, to see if you are among those who should not walk.

Walking for therapeutic purposes should only be done in close cooperation with the physician who is treating you and your physical therapist (see Walking During Convalescence, page 91).

English translation by Elizabeth Reinersmann
English translation edited by Isabel Stein.

Library of Congress Cataloging in Publication Data

Bös, Klaus.
    Walking for fitness & health / Klaus Bos ; [English translation by Elizabeth Reinersmann].
        p. cm.
    "Part of this work was originally published in Germany under the title Schlank, fit & gesund durch walking"—t. p. verso.
    ISBN 0–8069–9814–8
    1. Fitness walking. I. Bös, Klaus. Schlank, fit & gesund durch walking. English. II. Title.
    RA781.65.B67 1997
    613.7'176—dc21   97–35493
                                                                                CIP

10 9 8 7 6 5 4 3 2 1

Published by Sterling Publishing Company, Inc.
387 Park Avenue South, New York, N.Y. 10016
Part of this work was originally published in Germany under
the title *Schlank, fit & gesund durch Walking*
© 1995 by Gräfe und Unzer Verlag GmbH, München
English translation and new material
copyright © 1997 by Sterling Publishing Co.
Distributed in Canada by Sterling Publishing
c/o Canadian Manda Group, One Atlantic Avenue, Suite 105
Toronto, Ontario, Canada M6K 3E7
Distributed in Great Britain and Europe by Cassell PLC
Wellington House, 125 Strand, London WC2R 0BB, England
Distributed in Australia by Capricorn Link (Australia) Pty Ltd.
P.O. Box 6651, Baulkham Hills, Business Centre, NSW 2153, Australia
Manufactured in the United States of America
All rights reserved

Sterling ISBN 0-8069-9814-8

Contents

Preface   8

Introduction   9

Walking: Fun on the Go   11

Step by Step to Better Health   12
Walking Is Popular   12
What Is Walking?   13
Walking, Surrounded by Nature   14
Health Seen in Its Entirety   15
Health Through Gentle Endurance Training   15

What Are the Effects of Walking?   17
Strengthening the Heart and Circulation   17
Reducing Daily Stress   18
Slimming and Weight Loss   19

Walking: A Sport for Everyone?   20
Risk-Assessment Test Before Walking   20
Walking: A Must for Many   21
When to Avoid Walking   21
Is Walking Better Than Jogging or Hiking?   22

Training Tips for Walkers

Training Tips for Walkers · 25

Before You Start Walking · 26
The Right Clothing · 27
The Right Shoes · 28
Outdoor Walking and Ozone · 29
It Goes Better with Music · 30
Walk Regularly · 32
Walking as a Basic Routine · 33

Breathing and Walking Tempo · 34
Your Breathing Rhythm · 35
Find Your Walking Tempo · 36
Heart Rate and Walking Speed · 37
How Often and How Long to Walk · 39
Know Your Limits · 41

The Physical Fitness Self-Test · 43
What Is Your Endurance Level? · 43
Correct Walking Technique · 43
The Walking Test · 46
Evaluating the Walking Test · 48
Find Your Walking Program · 53

The Walking Programs · 57

Exercises for Feeling Good and Having Fun · 58
Warming Up Body and Mind · 58
The Warm-up Exercises · 61

Quick Relief for Back Pain · 68
Hip and Lower Back Exercises · 69
Exercises for the Shoulders and Upper Back · 72

Basic Walking Programs · 76
Testing the Waters: for Beginners · 77

Walking Programs for Advanced Walkers   79
Power Walking for the Ambitious   80

Special Walking Programs   82
Relaxing with Body-Conscious Walking   82
Walking Program for Older People   85
Slimming and Weight Loss Through Walking   87
Walking During Convalescence   91
When the Weather Is Bad   93
Indoor Gymnastics Program   94

Indoor Walking on the Treadmill   99
Walking Indoors, Whatever the Weather   100
Why Use a Treadmill?   101
What to Look for in a Treadmill   103
Is a Home Treadmill for You?   105
Indoor Walking Program for the Treadmill   106
Beginning Walking on the Treadmill
and Taking the Walking Test   107
Men's Ideal Weights, by Height and Frame   108
Women's Ideal Weights, by Height and Frame   109
Acknowledgments and Photo Credits   109
Index   111

Preface

Over the last few years, walking as a sport has become widely accepted. Young and old, healthy people and convalescents, thin people and those who are not so thin, all are walking actively on a regular basis, alone and in groups, and enjoying nature. In light of the fact that most of us are not nearly as active as we should be in our daily lives, this is a very positive development.

Walking has many health benefits and encourages social interaction. This book discusses walking in practical terms:

- What we mean by walking and who can benefit from this endurance sport
- How walking benefits the body, mind, and spirit
- How to breathe properly while walking
- How to take a walking test and practice walking techniques
- Which one of the eight walking programs is best for you.

A warm-up program, a special back-strengthening program, and an indoor treadmill walking program round out this comprehensive book.

Introduction

Walking can restore you to health or keep you healthy. You can begin walking at any age and continue as long as you enjoy doing something relaxing outdoors. You can walk alone, with your children, your parents, or with friends who want to add this activity to their lives.

Walking is excellent conditioning training, which is perhaps why it already has become a popular sport. It increases your health and well-being step by step and helps you to get a figure you feel comfortable with—an important point.

In the context of this book, walking means moving forward forcefully; the tempo is determined by your present condition. The techniques of exercise walking are easy to learn; walking shoes and proper clothing are easy to find. A park, a trail, or a street without too much traffic usually is within easy reach. And if that is not so, this particular kind of walking can be done when shopping or on the way to work, or even on a treadmill. However, you will need a bit of of persistence, because only those who train on a regular basis will remain fit and healthy.

Walking vigorously at your own tempo

Everything you need to know in order to walk properly and have fun while you are doing it is presented in this book, including interesting facts about the effects of walking on well-being and mood, on the heart and the circulatory system, and on the muscles and joints. A self-evaluation test that will aid you in correctly gauging your present fitness level, warm-up exercises, and suggestions for choosing the correct program for you also are included. The choices are many: you will find a walking program for beginners, for more advanced walkers, for power walkers, for convalescents, for people over 70 years old, and for those who want to lose weight and slim down through walking and proper nutrition. A program for walking indoors on a treadmill also is included.

Walking programs

Make your walking program an integral part of your daily activity and set yourself goals that you can easily realize. We wish you much fun and hope you will not hesitate to get started.

Walking: Fun on the Go

Research has shown that people who do endurance sports live healthier, longer, and more enjoyably. One sport that promotes optimum endurance is walking. It is the ideal leisure-time, everyday sport because for the human body, walking is a natural form of motion. Regular walking keeps body, mind, and spirit healthy and fit, increases a person's level of resilience, and improves the emotional state, all in a gentle way. Walking is subject to no internal or external performance pressure. Walking has nothing to do with high achievement, as is the case in competitive sports. Rather, through the routine of walking briskly, the body experiences the pleasure of movement.

Step by Step to Better Health

Walking is more than a new fad, more than a trendy sport that will fade away in a short time. Walking is an endurance sport that can be enjoyed for a whole lifetime. In the U.S., walking long ago passed jogging as the favorite fitness-building activity.

Walking is fun

The explosive growth in the number of people who walk, in the courses being taught on the subject, and in the walking groups being formed can only be explained by one fact: walking is great fun, even for the most stalwart couch potato, once he or she gives walking a try. Walking can move the most adamant opponent of athletic activities and is for people of every age.

Walking Is Popular

Walking as a sport is in fashion. In the comic movie *When Harry Met Sally*, we see Harry and Sally walking in the park, vigorously swinging their arms, discussing the problems in their relationship. In Central Park in New York, stressed-out managers are part of the everyday scene: with cellular phones tucked into their belts, they keep themselves fit by walking. They are combining an appreciation of nature and their surroundings with a special body experience. Gone are the times where we where told, "No pain, no gain," when we believed you had to crawl on all fours out the door of the body-building studio for your training to really be worth it.

Rediscover nature and your surroundings

The goal of walking is health, well-being, and strength. Walking as a gentle, relaxing way to be fit, to nourish your body, mind, and spirit is good for all the following people:

• Beginners and those starting over again who are looking for a healthy and appropriate way to exercise
• Those who want to be healthy but are asking: Do I have to kill myself for it?

- Athletes recovering from injuries, for whom jogging puts too much stress on the joints and slows down the healing process
- People in physical therapy who want to regain or increase their former performance levels and fitness
- Older people who want to retain or even increase their vitality, mobility, and the quality of their lives
- People who want to slim down and take control of their weight.

Walking is fun and improves your health

What Is Walking?

The word *walking* simply means "moving on foot." But walking is more than just going from place to place on foot. In our context, walking means moving briskly, athletically, in one of several different ways.

As far as speed is concerned, one can walk leisurely or briskly, meditatively or for relaxation, or power walk, carrying weights.

However, do not confuse walking as discussed here with the competitive sport of race walking. In the latter, performance and training are governed by international standards. The emphasis for us is on personal fitness and goals. Although the walking tech-

Don't walk
with exag-
gerated hip
movements
niques are similar to those practiced in competitive race walking, the main difference is that our walking methods do not include the extreme hip movements that race walkers use in order to increase their speed.

Walking, Surrounded by Nature

Walking is known as a gentle sport practiced for health. What it means to be fit and healthy is described by an enthusiastic walker:

> Ever since I starting walking, I simply feel better. I always hated to get up in the morning. I always felt worn out before I even got about of bed—as if I had no energy. My physician wanted to prescribe medication to combat my bad mood and my headaches. No deal, I told myself! I could get sick just from the side effects of the medicine. And then I read that walking is supposed to be a gentle sport and that I could take a class where interested people go to find out if walking is for them. Well, I tried it out. The class has long come to an end, I am sorry to say. But some students have kept in touch: I now meet two people from my class regularly every Saturday at noon in our park. I would never want to miss the hour outside close to nature....

This example tells you how health works. Here is a woman in her middle years, an executive secretary by profession, stressed out because of time pressure and the hectic pace in her life. She feels stressed and without energy. She is unhappy with herself, perhaps including with her body, which is showing age-related changes. She has become a stranger to herself, has lost a sense of herself. She is tired and can't get going. She feels that something has to be done; she can't continue like this any longer.

Walking
frequentl

The advice from her physician to try an antidepressant gave her the necessary impetus to change. Of course, she knows the positive effects sports have on health. In trying out walking, she discovered an enthusiasm that won't diminish. In the process she is experiencing an increase in well-being and new satisfaction.

Health Seen in Its Entirety

Health is a fleeting condition that changes constantly. While our language talks about health only in the singular, by now medical science has identified more than 60 000 illnesses! To this day, all attempts to find a universally accepted definition of health have been unsatisfactory. Traditionally, when doctors talk about health, they talk about the absence of illness. But would you consider a highly trained athlete who has established world records but suffers from a chronic knee problem to be a sick person? What about a person with a disability who, while not able to walk, is nevertheless living life enthusiastically? The phenomenon *health* can therefore only be considered in its entirety. A human being is made up of body, mind, and a spirit that together represent the whole person. Today we are rediscovering the age-old image of a human being: body, mind, and spirit are one. The World Health Organization (WHO) has expressed and idealized this in its definition of health: "Health is not only the absence of illness but rather a condition of total physical, psychological, and spiritual well-being" (WHO, 1987).

Body, mind, and spirit are one

Let's take as an example the words of the enthusiastic walker on page 14: in a medical sense she was not sick; if anything, she just felt weak. But she felt uncomfortable psychologically and spiritually and was dissatisfied with herself. Through walking, she improved not only her psychological state, but also her social life.

Health Through Gentle Endurance Training

The things that affect our health, fitness, vitality and well-being negatively or positively are well known. Habits like smoking, using alcohol in excess, lack of exercise, and too much or the wrong kind of food endanger and harm our health. These habits are risk factors and are the main reason for many of our health problems—for instance, heart attacks or cancer.

Positive effects

Exercise (particularly endurance sports), healthy diet, and active relaxation maintain or improve your fitness level and the well-being of body, mind, and spirit.

**Health-
protecting
factors**

Medical science and sports science have agreed for some time now on the positive effects of endurance training: we should burn an additional 1000 to 2000 calories each week through physical or athletic activities in order to prevent heart disease, for instance. Swimming, skiing, biking, and, above all, running are recommended. However, the risks inherent in the traditional endurance sports have so far been overlooked. Recent studies have shown that excessive endurance training, usually due to unrealistic goals or false pride, can diminish memory and weaken the immune system. That's without even mentioning all the athletes in the offices of orthopedic surgeons because of the damage they have done to their joints and bones.

**Gentle
endurance
training**

The advantage of walking as endurance training is that the positive effects of endurance training are enhanced with less effort, less stress, and without the wear and tear on the body that running causes. And this happens in a gentle way: walking—the gentle way to health.

What Are the Effects of Walking?

Results of research on walking have shown its many healing effects.

Strengthening the Heart and Circulation

Exercise on a regular basis makes your heart slower and stronger. This is an important fact, because it lowers the risk of overtaxing the heart muscle. This is similar to a motor: when it runs at a lower number of rpm (rotations per minute), it is less likely to develop problems. The heart muscle becomes better supplied with blood and gets more oxygen. More blood per heartbeat is pumped into the arteries. More blood means more oxygen and more energy-producing substances to the organs.

The heart becomes stronger

• Your blood can take in more oxygen when you are at rest or asleep. This leads to better maintenance of the organs.
• Your lungs become larger. The volume of air and therefore the oxygen intake is increased.
• Your muscles become stronger and more flexible. Muscle cells increase in size and increase the number of energy-storage sites and calorie-burning centers which, in turn, increases energy consumption, using up carbohydrates and fats taken in as food.
• Bones, joints, tendons, and ligaments become stronger and more resilient. Susceptibility to injuries and premature wear and tear is reduced; muscle cramping happens less frequently.

Fitness level increases

Summarizing the positive physical effects of walking: a measurable increase in the level of fitness—physically, mentally, and emotionally.

Reducing Daily Stress

Walking is a good antidote for the stresses of modern life. Tension, anxiety, impatience, jittery nerves, anger, apathy, irritability, and fear influence our autonomic nervous system, which usually is beyond our control, and can result in physical symptoms like dizziness, labored breathing, rapid pulse, and headaches. When you walk, antistress hormones are released into the bloodstream, which help alleviate or lessen these symptoms. The result is better emotional balance and stability.

Increase in self-confidence

In addition, psychological and sociological studies have established that people who walk have more self-confidence when compared to those that are not involved in any sport. The trust in one's own abilities in many areas grows in direct relationship to the general improvement in fitness achieved through walking. Walkers are also known for their extraordinary ability to make friends.

Walking for peace of mind

Slimming and Weight Loss

Walking is the optimal endurance sport if you want to become slim and trim or stay that way without strenuous efforts. Walking works by burning the body's fat deposits. Through a sustained, gentle, and easy stress load over a specific time and with a specific amount of intensity, the body's fat provides the energy needed for walking. While the intensity of walking should be kept as low as possible, it should nevertheless be high enough so that there is a sufficient amount of oxygen available for the energy processes occurring in muscles.

Walking burns fat

Follow This Rule of Thumb About Walking Speed

■ The rule of thumb in walking is: Walk without getting out of breath. If you do, you are walking too fast. Rapid breathing or gasping for air is a sign that your body lacks the necessary oxygen because you are going too fast. Therefore take this rule to heart when you are training: as long as you can keep up a conversation, your tempo is okay. This is particularly important when you are walking uphill.

If you keep this in mind, your fat deposits will disappear in no time. Fat metabolism sets in within minutes after you start walking, so you have the necessary energy. After 45 minutes, fat metabolism is the main energy deliverer. Tell yourself you will walk 45 minutes every day. You will see for yourself how fast fat will change into firm muscles. Walking reshapes your body.

Walking: A Sport for Everyone?

Ask your doctor

Walking, as we stated before, is appropriate for all age groups. There is hardly a person who could not simply get up and go. But still, there are people with certain physical symptoms who should not walk under any circumstances. These people ought to talk to their family doctor and make sure that even a gentle walk does not present a risk.

Before you start walking, please take this Risk-Assessment Test.

Risk-Assessment Test Before Walking

Do you have an irregular pulse?	Yes	No
Do you have joint problems?	Yes	No
Have you been hospitalized within the last year?	Yes	No
Are you sick now or do you have a fever?	Yes	No

■ If you have answered *yes* to even one of the above questions, you absolutely must consult your physician to find out if walking is right for you.

Avoid health risks

■ Do not walk with a fever (above 100°F or 38°C), or a respiratory infection, cold or cough. It could result in lung or heart muscle inflammation in no time. This warning should not be taken lightly.

Walking: A Must for Many

The following people should start on a walking program:

People
who
should
walk

• People who sit for more than 9 hours a day
• People who are on their feet for more than 9 hours a day
• People who usually are outdoors less than 15 minutes a day
• People who climb fewer than 25 stairs a day
• People who do sports for less than 30 minutes a week
• People whose breathing becomes labored when they walk or climb stairs fast
• People who experience joint discomfort when sitting or lying down
• People who experience tension in their back muscles and/or neck and shoulder muscles
• People who have a high resting pulse (higher than 80 beats per minute)
• People who are overweight, which means: at least 10% above the ideal for their height (see the tables on pages 108 and 109 to find out what your ideal weight should be).

If one or more of the above applies to you, it is high time to become active, because it shows a definite lack of exercise.

When to Avoid Walking

Do not walk you have the following illnesses or symptoms:

People for
whom
walking is
a risk

• Severe circulatory problems that cause limb pain while you rest
• If you can't walk more than 100 yards (100 m) without experiencing pain
• If you have unstable angina pectoris, meaning that you have chest pains that change or radiate to the left side of your body, accompanied by breathing difficulties. This might be a warning signal of an impending heart attack!
• If you have high blood pressure—namely, yours is consistently above 140/90 mm Hg
• Severe heart irregularity that is accompanied by breathing difficulties and chest plain, as well as severe coronary artery stenosis.

Get a
check-up
from your
doctor We'd rather see you checking up with your physician one time too
often than one time too few. Get a comprehensive medical check-
up before you start your walking program. Practicing prevention
now is better than having regrets later!

Is Walking Better Than Jogging or Hiking?

Hiking is a popular pastime. If you want to achieve the same
benefits from hiking that you get from walking, you need to
hike at least 10 km (6.2 mi) every weekend. The difference
between walking and hiking is that the former is more economi-
cal, which means that because it is a goal-oriented athletic activity, you achieve the results in less time. Walking in a group lets
you meet new, like-minded people and allows you to build
friendships and exchange experiences—all in all, a rather important social aspect. Furthermore, walking is much easier to incorporate in your everyday life than hiking. Jogging as an endurance
sport has the same beneficial effects as walking. In the face of the
big jogging movement that already exists, it would be pretty pre-
sumptuous of us to think that we can lure committed joggers away
from their sport. But compared
to walking, jogging has its risks.
Based on the observations of
orthopedic surgeons, who see an
ever-increasing number of ankle,
knee, and hip joint problems
and athletic injuries, we begin to
understand that some sports can
be dangerous.

*Walking
is more
effective
than
hiking*

In jogging, as in many other
types of endurance sports, some
people tend to train too intensely, too often simply because of
misplaced pride, paying no
attention to the body's signals:
"Stop! I am hurting!" Joint
pains are ignored although they

*Walking:
a real
alternative
to jogging*

are a sign of overload. The well-meant advice that jogging is good for your health has led to the widespread belief that more is better. But this is far from the truth. Sensible and responsible use of one's body also means that the chosen sport should be carried out in a healthy way. We would like to turn the above phrase around to say: "Less is better." We hope to find many supporters of this slogan.

Avoid false pride

The Alternative to Jogging

Walking is a true alternative to jogging. If, as a jogger, you increasingly experience joint pains, why not take a closer look at walking as a sport. If, on the other hand, you have started to jog and have given up after a short time because it seems too hard, try walking, either alone or in a walking group; one might already exist in your neighborhood.

Walking in a group

Training Tips for Walkers

You can walk almost everywhere: in a park, along a highway or country road, to the post office or the supermarket. It is the most practical of all the training programs available. Walking can be done almost anytime and in any weather, no matter where you happen to be, and in another form at home or when on vacation. The only thing that you need is to remember is: whether walking or jogging, do it without getting out of breath. If you're short of breath, you're going too fast. With the help of the walking self-test in this chapter, you can easily determine your fitness level. Choose the appropriate walking program, depending on the result of your physical fitness check-up at the doctor's and your self-test in this chapter, and then train accordingly.

Before You Start Walking

"There is no such thing as bad weather, only the wrong clothing." This saying could have been coined for outdoor walking. Only when it rains "cats and dogs" or temperatures are extreme should walking outdoors be suspended. For bad-weather days, we have put together a special indoor gymnastic program that you can use at home. You can also use a treadmill at a health club or at home. In the treadmill chapter are tips on how to use a treadmill and suggestions on how to design a walking program around it.

When the weather is bad, exercise at home

Before you start walking, we have a few suggestions:

• Reread the discussion on breathing and walking techniques (see pages 34 to 36) and the part about how to check your heart rate (pulse; page 37).
• Tips from experienced walkers are often very valuable and in the beginning can greatly increase your enjoyment.
• The Physical Fitness Self-Test (page 43) will aid you in creating your own individual program.

Tips from experienced walkers

Walk 10 to 20 Minutes Every Day

People who wear conventional clothing—suits, shirt and tie, or blouses because of their professions—should nevertheless try to walk briskly on their way to work. Ten to twenty minutes of daily walking is sufficient to balance sitting or standing at work. An early walk will also let you start the day more alert and prepare you optimally for the mental stresses of the day. If you tend to perspire easily, a good deodorant can help. You will discover that walking home after a stressful day on the job will let you arrive ready for well-deserved relaxation.

The Right Clothing

You do not need any particular type of clothing or accessories for walking. If you are only able to walk during your lunch break or on the way to and from work, we recommend you wear clothing in which you feel comfortable.

Clothing made of cotton

Light cotton clothing is best. As far as shoes are concerned, any will do except those with high heels.

For your regular walking sessions, you might want to invest in a comfortable athletic suit or leisure suit that allows you to move freely. They are made of easy-care fibers and are easy to launder.

If the weather is cool, it's better to wear one or two light sweatshirts over your T-shirt, rather than a heavy jacket. Remember that your skin is, as far as surface area is concerned, the largest breathing organ of your body. A lined jacket should only be worn when it is bitter cold or when a chilling wind is blowing. At any other time, it is simply unnecessary ballast. Sweatshirts, on the other hand, can easily be tied around the waist whenever you get too hot.

Rain gear, ponchos and jackets, are easy to find and

This rain-proof jacket is very practical

allow you to walk in any weather. Garments made of fabrics that breathe prevent rain from penetrating the fabric and allow perspiration to cool the skin, while letting body heat pass to the outside. As a general rule, this type of clothing is a bit more expensive than regular rain gear or windbreakers.

The Right Shoes

Walking shoes are the beginning and end of basic equipment for walking. The kind of shoes you choose determines how comfortable you will be when you walk.

Shoes are the quintessential item for walking. The choice of proper shoes will decide if your feet and joints feel good while you walk. When shopping for shoes, you should not skimp on money or time. Several different kinds of jogging and running shoes have been developed for endurance sports.

Take your time when buying shoes

Because of their light and flexible style and their shock-absorbing soles, they are particularly good when you must do your walking on hard surfaces, like asphalt. Shoes that are not made exclusively from leather can even be washed in the washing machine in water as warm as 104°F (40°C).

A Short Checklist for Buying Shoes

1. Buy shoes with a built-in shock-absorbing system, like like air or gel-filling. These shoes will prevent or lessen stress on joints and ligaments.

2. Don't buy shoes that are too small; most people buy their walking shoes one size larger than their regular shoes. This will prevent undue pressure on the feet and allow for adequate movement.

3. Let a physician or sales person advise you as to what kind of feet you have and which kind of shoes are appropriate for your feet; then try on what has been recommended. Special shoes can be made for you if your feet turn in or out.

Seek professional advice when buying shoes

Our Shoe Tips

For the achievement-oriented walker, we recommend the purchase of walking shoes that have been specifically designed for this particular walking technique. They come with an extremely sloped heel, give maximum support for the heel, and reduce the time your feet roll forward. Push-off action from the ground is helped by a raised section under the ball of the foot. This elevated part makes it easier for the foot to be catapulted forward. You will move with the speed of a fire engine. For the power walker, these shoes are a must.

Outdoor Walking and Ozone

Let air and sunshine touch your skin; it will thank you for it. But protect yourself from the dangers of ultraviolet rays. A lotion with the appropriate sun protection factor (SPF) is absolutely essential.

Don't walk at high noon
Do not walk in the burning midday sun and heat. The cooler times of the morning or early in the evening are better, not only because that is when ozone levels are at their lowest.

■ A note about the environment: use your car as little as possible for going to work, after work, and on vacations. Use public transportation, your bicycle, or walk.

Walking in Parks and Forests

Parks, meadows, forests, and tree-lined trails are ideal places for walking. Here you have the best chance to find good air, quiet, and seclusion.

Being surrounded by nature stimulates all your senses: the air caresses your skin and hair; meadows, shrubs, and trees in the forest invite you to discover with your eyes and ears the plant and animal life around you. You will hear the varied sounds of leaves moving in the air and all the different songs of the birds, all this while you are gently and rhythmically walking along. Pay attention to how you feel inside, how the air moves into and through your body and how new energies are flowing through you. Open your mind and your soul and become part of the environment. This will, without a

Walking awakens all your senses

Important Facts About Ozone

Ozone close to the surface of the earth is an irritating gas that is created from the reaction of automobile exhaust and strong sunlight. The main producers of ozone are automobiles and industry. Ozone readings have dramatically increased over the last years, particularly during the summer months. Many people experience breathing problems as a result of ozone. For that reason, do not walk on days when ozone readings are high. But if lunchtime is absolutely the only time when you can walk, stay as far away from streets and places with high traffic as you can. You probably can get ozone level readings at the local Environmental Protection Agency office or public health department.

doubt, make every walk an unforgettable experience.

The Condition of the Surface

Try to find a surface that is flat and solid. The condition of the surface you are walking on determines your rhythm and tempo. For that reason, trails covered with loose gravel or sand are not all that good. The surface of forest trails is ideal; it is usually resilient and smooth, especially in evergreen forests or in the fall, when it is dry and the trails are covered with leaves. We highly recommend walking on the beach at

water's edge, where the sand is compact. If you can, walk barefoot; you will get a gentle massage in the process and it is free. A real bargain!

On loose sand and grass, walk with your shoes on

Barefoot at water's edge

It Goes Better with Music

While you walk, imagine that your breath is music, flowing through your body, circulating and pulsating through every organ. If you like, you might also take along an audiocassette player. Fast-paced music like rock 'n' roll is a good motivator for power walking and race walking; music with a slower tempo, like classical sonatas and symphonies, soul, or blues, on the other hand are good for a relaxing and meditative walk.

Weights to exercise the upper body

Stores carry tapes and discs for educational purposes and music specifically for the

ducational and music audio- cassettes

walker; these are made for the beginner as well as advanced and power walkers. In addition to portable cassette player, you can also purchase walking exercise tapes for strengthening yourself. Of course, you can also create your own music program.

We leave it up to your imagination to choose among the many accessories available in specialty shops. In the beginning, when walking was still a new development and

had only a few followers, people walked without any specific equipment. Today, fitness-hungry walkers carry small weights to give the upper body a workout. Some people carry specifically designed and weighted backpacks, increasing the effects of their training. Imagination knows no boundaries. Everything that is fun is alright, as long as it does not overtax you.

Caution

Don't walk in traffic while listening to audiocassettes. If your ears are covered, use your eyes to watch out for cars and people.

Walk Regularly

Walking is an endurance sport that you can enjoy regardless of the time of year or day. Wearing the appropriate clothing allows you to walk in almost any season. The healthy effects on body, mind, and spirit, however, will only come when you walk on a regular basis.

Take Your Time!

In our beginner's walking courses, people never fail to tell us that they couldn't possibly walk on a regular basis. Our own experience, however, has shown that lack of time, being tired, or bad weather often are simply nothing more than excuses. Might the real reason be lack of interest or inertia? This could also be a case of: "The spirit is strong, but the body is weak." Why not turn it around. Be more motivated and say: "Where there is a will, there is a way!"

Training and following an exercise program properly means looking at your weaknesses, but most of all at your strengths, and arranging a walking regimen according to your personal goals and the time that you can budget into the day for it. You know yourself better than anybody else, and it is you who have to find out what it takes to make exercising fun and when is the most convenient time for your walk. Methodically organizing and planning your day usually lets you discover many empty times. Fill them with walking!

Add walking to your daily schedule

Make exercising fun

Walking as a Basic Routine

Weigh your everyday activities: ask yourself which one you can do without, which of your responsibilities could be relinquished and which not. On the top of such a list in importance should be preserving your health. "Health is not everything, but without it there is nothing." These are the words of the philosopher Arthur Schopenhauer. In the absence of active, healthy behavior, the quality of your life will surely diminish over time. So why don't you give **It pays** walking a try! You will soon **to try** find that walking has become a habit that you cannot break. After a certain time, your body will, as a matter of course, demand the right for gentle movement, because your body knows instinctively what is good for it.

Try to Walk 3 or 4 Times a Week

According to experts in sports medicine, walking as an exer-cise is most beneficial when done three to four times a week for about 45 to 60 minutes each session. Coordinate your walking times with the rest of your day's activities and plan your schedule at the beginning of the week. Enter your walking times into your calendar just as you do other appointments: hairdresser or barber shop, going to the movies, or meeting friends. Then walking will be equally as important and indispensable as your other activities. It is worth devoting one hour a day (including a shower and changing clothes) to your health.

Build walking into your daily routine

Breathing and Walking Tempo

Lungs continually process air. From the moment of birth, our lungs draw in life-sustaining oxygen, and thus energy, with every breath. Our bodies are incapable of storing oxygen as they do fat. Oxygen must be supplied continuously through respiration. An equally important part of breathing is the exhalation of carbon dioxide, a by-product of the energy-producing process within our cells. This activity occurs in two places:

• Between the alveoli in the lungs and the blood flowing through them (external respiration)

• Between individual cells in the body and blood (internal respiration).

With every heartbeat, oxygen is taken up by alveoli and transported to the body's organs, where it is used up. The blood then carries the carbon dioxide back to the alveoli, where it is exhaled.

Oxygen intake and consumption and exhalation of carbon dioxide are normally in balance, called the steady state.

Through walking, we take more oxygen into our lungs, because we need more oxygen than when resting. We can get the extra oxygen we need when walking by inhaling and exhaling faster (increased breathing frequency) or by breathing more deeply. If there is too much carbon dioxide in the blood and too little oxygen, breathing automatically becomes deeper, followed by an increase in frequency.

When walking, we want to sustain the dynamics of the steady state and strengthen the breathing process.

Walking is the type of endurance sport that gently stimulates the body aerobically, which means with the help of oxygen. By keeping our breath at a steady rhythm, we can balance the excess of carbon dioxide and the lack of oxygen that is created when we walk.

Your Breathing Rhythm

Breathing frequency and depth increase

The slight increase in effort when walking increases your normal breathing, something that happens automatically. Because your body needs more oxygen, you begin to take deeper breaths. People who aren't fit, compared to physically fit ones, get out of breath much faster. This is a sign that your muscles and your breathing apparatus need to be strengthened. During intense physical exertion—for instance, during a sprint—your muscles are unable to take up a sufficient amount of oxygen if you are not fit. Oxygen is exhaled unused. Muscles work without enough oxygen. The result is muscles that tire very quickly. The body's endurance is quickly diminished.

■ Getting out of breath when you walk is a sign that you are going too fast.

■ You can support the breathing process actively by breathing in and out deeply and evenly and in rhythm with your steps: inhale through the nose and exhale through the mouth. In this way, the air you breathe in reaches the alveoli in the lungs already warmed up, humidified, and cleansed by passing through your nose.

■ Try to find your breathing rhythm. Experiment with inhaling for three steps and exhaling for the next three steps. If more oxygen is needed by your body, you may alternate between inhaling through the nose and the mouth.

■ If you are still gasping for air after trying the above, start slowing down and then stop. With the following breathing exercise, you will recover quickly and soon be able to continue your walk.

Stop if you have to gasp for air

Breathing exercise, step 1

Breathing exercise, step 2

Breathing Exercise

• Without lifting your shoulders, move your bent arms up in front of your body (see left photo above)
• Push your arms down at the same time that you you exhale (see right photo above).

Exhalation expels carbon dioxide from the body. The organism is then again able to quickly take up oxygen, transferring it via the bloodstream to the muscles, and balance the oxygen deficit. This breathing exercise relieves the side pain that often appears during walking. The pain is a sign of a lack of oxygen somewhere—for instance, in the liver. It is there

that body fats and sugars, and things needed for muscle energy, are converted into usable form. If the liver does not have enough oxygen during physical exertion, it signals through pain and cramping that it cannot keep up with the oxygen conversion.

Find Your Walking Tempo

Breathing is influenced by internal and external processes. But sometimes we are mislead by false sensations.

For instance, sometimes we are unaware that we are overtaxed, which happens when our bodies do not send a clear message or we have not learned how to pay attention to the messages that are being sent. When you are out of breath, check your heart rate.

Heart Rate and Walking Speed

Heart rate and walking

Depending on your age, gender, level of fitness, and your constitution, your resting heart normally beats 60 to 80 times a minute (your heart rate), and pushes between 5 to 7 liters (5 to 7 quarts) of blood through the arteries. Depending on the intensity of physical exercise, the heart rate can increase to 180 beats per minute during walking. Heart rate, then, is an indication of the level of physical intensity of a given exercise. After many studies, sports physicians have determined which heart rates can safely be sustained and cause health benefits during a particular workout. Of course, there are deviations from these values that have to do with body weight. But the rule of thumb given above, right, has been established for men as well as women.

• You are walking at the proper tempo when you stay within your target heart rate range. You will probably notice during

The Rule of Thumb Is:

1. Take 220 beats per minute (S), and subtract your age in years (A).

2. Take 75% to 80% of the result. Your answer is the target training heart rate (in beats per minute) for you during exercise.

the course of regular training that you can suddenly walk faster, while still staying within your desired heart rate range. This is the first physically noticeable increase in your endurance level as a result of your training.

Practice checking your heart rate

To Find Your Optimal Training Heart Rate Range for Walking (for Men or Women)

Age	Max. Heart Rate* (beats/min.)	Training Range** (beats/min.)
20	200	150 to 160
25	195	146 to 156
30	190	143 to 152
35	185	139 to 148
40	180	135 to 144
45	175	131 to 140
50	170	128 to 136
55	165	124 to 132
60	160	120 to 128
65	155	116 to 124
70	150	113 to 120

*220 minus age in years.
**75% to 80% of maximum heart rate
A 30-year-old man therefore should train with a range of 143–152 heartbeats per minute; a 60-year-old woman, with a range of 120–128 beats per minute.

How to Measure Your Heart Rate

It is almost impossible to measure your heart rate while walking, unless you have a heart-rate monitor. Before you start walking, practice taking your pulse. It is not easy to find it and count your heart beats after you have started to walk, are out of breath, and your pulse is racing.

Measuring the heart rate at the wrist

■ This is how its done:

• You need a watch with a second hand for measuring your heart rate. Always stop walking when measuring your heart rate.
• Measure your heart rate on the forearm at the artery just above the wrist. Apply slight pressure with your index, middle, and ring finger on the place between the wrist bone and the ligaments in the center of your arm on the thumb side of your wrist. Can you feel your pulse?
• As soon as you have found your heartbeat, look at the second hand of your watch and count the heart beat for 15 seconds. Multiply that number by

4 and you will have the heart rate per minute.

If your heart rate is above the optimal training range (see page 38), wait until your heart rate has slowed down; if it is below the optimum range, you can walk a little faster.

Pay attention to the signals that your body is sending you. Your body is in balance if you feel well and comfortable during your walk and afterwards; if your breath is slow, deep, and quiet; if you have no joint or muscle difficulties and your training heart rate is in the optimal range. Find your proper tempo every time you walk.

Pay attention to your body's signals

How Often and How Long to Walk

Frequency and duration of your weekly walks depends on how fit you are at the time. Allow enough time for recovery between each outing. Your body needs to rest so that it can take advantage of the health-improving routine.

My training heart rate is between ☐ *and* ☐ *beats/min.*

Start Gently: Increase Slowly

If you have not been involved in any athletic or physical activities for many years, we recommend that you limit each session to about 30 minutes once a week for the first 4 to 5 weeks. In addition, you should do a short exercise program once a week (see page 68). Read the specific walking program that applies to you for details of sessions' length and frequency.

Don't overdo it in the beginning

■ Only after completing this initial phase should you walk twice a week. A pause of two days between outings is ideal. In this way, you are slowly increasing and stabilizing your fitness level. Only after walking regularly for 6 months should you increase to three and later to four days a week. The duration of each walk is slowly increased, based on your improving physical condition. After about 12 weeks, you may want to extend your walk to 45 minutes, and after 6 months, you can walk for 60 minutes.

■ A slow but steady increase in your training assures that the fitness you have achieved will be more stable than it would be if you were working out intensely for a short period of time. It seems that our bodies remember how they have been treated. Our bodies are grateful if physical demands are subtle and gentle!

Recuperating Between Outings

Take a break

After an hour-long walk, your body, generally speaking, is pleasantly fatigued and performs less efficiently. Time is needed to compensate and balance the system so it can regain its normal capacities. The amount of time depends on the level of fatigue. The only important goal for those who work out for health reasons (and walkers count themselves in this category) is to achieve and maintain an optimum level of physical fitness.

Beginners, or those who are reentering the sport, will notice that improvements in fitness level happen quickly. But here, too, caution is advised, because the heart and circulatory systems and the neuromuscular system adapt much faster to the demands of walking than do other parts of the body, like tendons, ligaments, cartilage, and bones.

• Do not forget: only a

fully rested body can increase its level of fitness above what it was at the outset. When you properly balance rest with the physical exertion of walking you will truly feel invigorated and good.

Know Your Limits

Not everybody is resilient and fit. After a long, unavoidable interruption due to injury or illness, or if more than 6 months have elapsed since you have been physically active, you must start your walking **Be 40 but** program very carefully.
remain 20

To be fit or become fit means for many older people to be young again and stay young. Sports medicine doctors are fond of saying: "Be 40 but remain 20." And they are right. Not all difficulties and risks can be eliminated by walking, but it has been documented without a question that walking does increase the quality of life. For that reason, start slowly and on a sensible schedule; you have all the time in the world.

Pain, the Body's Warning Signal

• Pay attention to warning signals; listen to your body! Pain

during or after a walk could be a sign that you have overdone it. If the pain does not go away or it returns, see your doctor and have a physical examination.

• Sometimes, joints start to ache after you have been physically inactive. This usu- **If you** ally disappears when you start **have** walking. If this is the case, **pains, go** moving is truly the best thing **to the** you can do. But keep an eye **doctor** on such symptoms.

• Never walk when you have an acute infection, fever, or a cold. While it is healthy to perspire, walking to sweat out an illness can have grave consequences. Most illnesses are harmless, but acute illnesses have caused lung and heart muscle infections that can be life-threatening.

One Step Forward, Two Back

■ Signs that you have overtaxed your system or increased the level of your exercises too fast are muscle or joint pain, stiff muscles, tiredness and exhaustion.

■ If your muscles or joints are sore, you should discontinue walking until the pain has disappeared.

Symptoms of over-exertion

■ Sharp pain—for instance in joint areas—can be lessened by cooling; for example, you can put an ice pack on the area.

■ Constant joint and muscle pain should be treated with heat: a hot shower, a heating pad, or infrared light. If pain persists, seek medical advice.

■ If you have sore muscles, wait until the pain subsides. Sore muscles should not be massaged. Superficial strokes with slight pressure is fine. Sore muscles are a sign that microfibers have been torn; this is painful but not serious. The injuries usually are healed after two days.

■ Tiredness and exhaustion can be signs of overtraining. They are signs that you have not left sufficient rest periods between walking sessions for the regeneration of your body. Over time, this can lower your fitness level, making you listless and feeling weak. Interrupt your walking training and get recharged! Give your body time to recuperate.

The Measure of Things Is You

Listen to your inner voice

Misplaced pride has been the undoing of many. Don't measure yourself by the performance of others or wish for super fitness. Establish your own, individual program and listen to your inner voice, because that voice will tell you what is good for your body.

The Physical Fitness Self-Test

Fitness means physical strength and agility. Physical strength is different for men and women and is closely related to age. Evaluating a person's level of fitness needs to be done specifically for that individual.

■ Technically, when we speak of exercising to improve health, we differentiate among four basic fitness qualities: endurance, strength, suppleness, and coordination, meaning the integration of the different phases of movement. Speed plays only a secondary role in walking; endurance, on the other hand, is the most important aspect.

What Is Your Endurance Level?

Using the walking test as an aid, you can determine your endurance level, the most important part of fitness and health. The walking test (page 46) has been designed and scientifically tested by sports medicine doctors specifically for walking. It is widely used in physical examinations for determining a person's endurance level. Taking the test is fun and can easily be incorporated into your walking routine, because walking is all you have to do.

But first let us show you step by step how to walk properly.

Correct Walking Technique

Over the years, all of us have developed our very own way of walking. The walking technique we are teaching here is different than our ordinary walking.

■ Pay attention to the specifics of this walking technique. Move through them one step at a time. Walk relaxed and smoothly, with your usual length of stride. Take your time.

■ Start by studying the steps and foot movement: first see how you walk for only a few steps, then over a short distance, and then as you walk a little faster at your normal tempo. Only after you have gone through this routine should you begin to incorporate the other elements of walking:

• With every step you take, touch the ground with the heel first (photo 1). Consciously roll the foot forward until the toes touch the ground (photo 2). Push off the ground vigorously with your toes; slight inward or outward turning of the foot is absolutely normal (photo 3).

• After you have become familiar with the way the heels touch the ground first, be sure that your knees are slightly bent as the sole of the foot rolls forward (photo 4). In other words, when setting the

3 *(top righ*t*)*: **Feet may** t **slightly in** **out.**

4 *(bottom* *right)*: **Kne** **slightly be**

1 *(top left):* **Walking** **heel first.** 2 *(bottom* *left):* **Toes** **touch the** **ground**

5: Hands in loosely closed fists

• Hands are lightly closed in soft fists (photo 5). A tight fist indicates cramping.

The walking technique movements are easy and quick to learn, because you are building on what you already do when you walk normally. You don't need to watch and check your technique constantly. Rather, as you begin walking in this new way, incorporate

Upright and relaxed— the right way to walk

heel on the ground and rolling the foot forward, do not straighten the leg.

• Walk with the upper body upright. Look ahead, not down to the ground, if possible. Carry your shoulders back, without being pulled up, so your chest is opened up wide. This will give you the necessary breath. It will also prevent shoulder, neck, and back muscles from tightening up.

• Your arms are an active part of every movement. They swing relaxed, in pendulum fashion, in rhythm with every step. Arm movements are pronounced: move your arms, with elbows bent at about 90°, rhythmically past the hips and up to shoulder level.

Arms swing like a pendulum while you walk

senses can take in the surroundings, and your spirit will
find peace.

The Walking Test

Do the 2 km (1.2 mi) walking
test outdoors if possible.
Specific instructions for indoor
walking tests are discussed in
point 9 below.

Before you start the walking test, you should have
comple-ted the Risk-
Assessment Test (page 20).
For those who have not been
involved in regular physical
activity, the Risk-Assessment
Test is a must. If you are not
quite sure if it's all right to
take the walking test, check
with your physician. We do
not recommend the walking
test for people over 70 years
old. For that group, we have
devised a special walking program (page 85). If, how-ever,
you are an older person and
still would like to test your
endurance with the walking
test, check with your physician first.

Be sure to take the Risk-Assessment Test if you have been inactive

different tempos and change
direction often. Experiment
with walking faster and slowing down again. Walk as if see-
ing yourself in slow motion
and follow that with a sudden
burst of speed. At other times,
try to walk backwards or side-
ways, uphill and then down-
hill. Such games will enhance
the learning process and your
sense of awareness. Sooner or
later, it will be your uncon-
scious that sets the pace. Your

1. What You Need for the Walking Test.

You need a watch with a second hand. We recommend a
stop-watch, because you have
to measure your walking time

The walking movements will become familiar very quickly

in minutes and seconds and take your test heart rate (heartbeats/minute; see page 39). Bring a pencil and a piece of paper.

2. Where to Take the Walking Test.

Look for a level surface in a park or forest, or go to an athletic field with a 400-meter (.24 mi) running track. Walk exactly 2000 meters (1.2 mi).

3. Do a Warm-up Before You Start.

Warm up before you start your test by walking for about 200 or 300 meters (.1 or .2 mile). See how fast you can walk. That gives you a sense of the appropriate tempo during the test. Then collect yourself once more before you get down to business.

4. On Your Mark, Get Set, Go!

Walk as fast as you can. Don't forget to note the starting time. You will really start to perspire. As soon as you are out of breath, you know that you are walking too fast; your pulse is too high. Slow down immediately!

5. Reaching the Goal.

2000 meters can seem like a long way. As soon as you reach the finish line, check the stopwatch and note the minutes and seconds that have elapsed since you started. Next, con- (text continues on page 50)

Evaluating the Results of the Walking Test (for Men)

Age	Duration of Walk (Minutes:Seconds)		
	Below average	Average	Above average
20	>15:15	13:45–15:15	<13:45
25	>15:30	14:00–15:30	<14:00
30	>15:45	14:15–15:45	<14:15
35	>16:00	14:30–16:00	<14:30
40	>16:15	14:45–16:15	<14:45
45	>16:30	15:00–16:30	<15:00
50	>16:45	15:15–16:45	<15:15
55	>17:00	15:30–17:00	<15:30
60	>17:15	15:45–17:15	<15:45
65	>17:45	16:15–17:45	<16:15
70	>18:15	16:45–18:15	<16:45

My time: _____ minutes _____ seconds.

> means "greater than"
< means "less than"

Evaluating the Results of the Walking Test (for Women)

Age	Duration of Walk (Minutes:Seconds)		
	Below average	Average	Above average
20	>17:15	15:45–17:15	<15:45
25	>17:22	15:52–17:22	<15:52
30	>17:30	16:00–17:30	<16:00
35	>17:37	16:07–17:37	<16:07
40	>17:45	16:15–17:45	<16:15
45	>17:52	16:22–17:52	<16:22
50	>18:00	16:30–18:00	<16:30
55	>18:07	16:37–18:07	<16:37
60	>18:15	16:45–18:15	<16:45
65	>18:30	17:00–18:30	<17:00
70	>18:45	17:15–18:45	<17:15

My time: _____ minutes _____ seconds.

> means "greater than"
< means "less than"

Walking times for men are evaluated differently than those for women

Evaluating the Walking Test

We have two separate tables for assessing the walking tests of men and women, although we have only one heart rate table for both men and women (see page 51). Why?

• Women by nature have less muscle mass and lower body weight than men. The size of the heart muscle, the heart volume (the amount of blood that can be pumped by the heart per beat), and therefore the the maximum capacity of oxygen intake depend on the size of the heart and the muscle to body mass ratio.

• Women therefore have by nature, corresponding to their physical constitution, smaller hearts and a lower heart blood volume.

• For the evaluation of the walking times for the test, the lower body weight and the somewhat lower level of endurance in women have already been taken into consideration. Women might reach the end of the test distance a little later than their male counterparts, but they do have nevertheless the same heart rates as men. As far as women are concerned, their heart rates are evaluated the same as those of the men, but the time for completing the test walk is evaluated on a different chart.

centrate on taking your pulse (see page 38): place your fingers on the inside of your arm above the wrist, look at the stop-watch, and count your heartbeats for 15 seconds. Write down the number; multiply it by 4. You now have the

Target Heart Rates for Men and Women

Age (Years)	Target Heart Rate (Beats/Minute)
20	160–190
25	156–185
30	152–181
35	148-176
40	144–171
45	140–166
50	136–162
55	132–157
60	128–152
65	124–147
70	120–143

We use the same chart to evaluate heart rates for men and women

My test heart rate: _____ beats per minute

Walking time and stress heart rate

heartbeats per minute. Remember, you can easily miscount when you are out of breath!

6. First Take a Break.

Take a rest and assess your walking test. You can enter your walking test time in the tables on pages 48 or 49 and your heart rate in the box above.

7. How Good Was Your Time?

The time it took you to complete the walking test depends on the level of your fitness, your age, and gender; men find the answers on page 48, and women on page 49. First, look for your age bracket. For each age group, there are three different walking times listed: the middle column lists the average times from a study group; to the left are the lower scores, and on the right are the higher scores. Where does your test time fall?

Test time and stress heart rate

8. Your Heart's Fitness Is Important.

The walking time alone is not enough for evaluating the test results. The walking time in relation to your stress heart rate is more important. Your heart rate is the guide for evaluating the walking test performance. Find your age bracket in the heart rate table on page 51. Is your heart rate higher or lower than the average heart rate for your age group? Only now can you evaluate your walking level properly.

9. The Indoor Walking Test on the Treadmill.

The indoor walking test is similar to the outdoor walking test. The walking distance is 2000 meters (1.2 miles); both walking time and heart rate are measured. The advantage of the treadmill test is that the measurements are very accurate.

The disadvantage is that you can take the test only after you have gained some treadmill experience and know what the proper starting speed is for you. In order to get used to the treadmill and to determine your speed, you need a warm-up phase as a pretest. It is important that you get a feel for the appropriate speed before you take the test. Small corrections can then be made during the course of the test.

Evaluation of your test results and the choice of the appropriate treadmill program are done with the help of the time and heart rate tables on pages 48, 49, and 51.

10. Results of the Walking Test

A. Your walking test time is above average and your heart rate is below the target rate (test heart rate low, test time fast). You are very fit! Your level of endurance is excellent!

B. Your walking test time is average, and your heart rate is higher than the target rate. You are still in good shape, but you must make more effort in order to achieve good test results.

Advantages and disadvantages of the test on the treadmill

Results of the Fitness Tests	
Endurance Level	**Walking Program**
Walking test level D	Beginners (testing the waters)
Walking test level B, C	Advanced walker
Walking test level A	Power walking

C. Your walking test time is average, but your heart rate is low. Your endurance is sufficient. Perhaps you didn't try very hard on the test? Maybe you started slowly? Our suggestion: repeat the walking test on the next day and try to walk faster.

D. Your walking test time is below average, and your heart rate is within the target range. Take advantage of what walking can offer you. It is your best opportunity to do something for yourself, your fitness, and your health.

Warning!

E. Your walking test time is poor and your heart rate is elevated. Caution: do not walk; see your physician first!

My walking test level is:
A B C D E

Find Your Walking Program

Now you know your fitness level. The result of your walking test will aid you in finding the walking program that is right for you.

A suitable program

■ **Testing the Waters for Beginners.** If your test score is D and you are less than 70 years old, start with the Testing the Waters Program for Beginners (page 77).

■ **Advanced Walkers Program.** If your walking test

Special Walking Programs

Target Group	Walking Program
People 70+ years old	Walking for older people
Body-conscious people	Body-conscious walking
Overweight people	Slimming and weight loss
People who are recuperating	Walking during convalescence
Home or health club walker	Indoor walking on the treadmill

Special programs

score is B or C and you are less than 70 years old, start with the Advanced Walkers Program (page 79).

■ **Power Walking for the Ambitious.** If your walking test score is A and you are less than 70 years old, start with the Walking Program for the Ambitious (page 80).

We have designed special walking programs for specific groups of people. Choose one of the following if it fits your situation.

■**Walking Program for Older People** (page 85). If you are more than 70 years old, this is probably the proper program for you.

■ **Body-Conscious Walking** (page 82). This program is for all people who want to walk for relaxation and meditate, letting the mind drift and concentrating on bodily sensations.

■ **Slimming and Weight Loss Through Walking** (page 87). A walking program with tips for losing weight and eating a balanced diet. Not only for those who want to lose weight, but for others who are interested.

■ **Walking During Convalescence** (page 91). This is a walking program for people who want to beome fit again after illness or injuries.

■ **Indoor Gymnastics Program** (page 94). When the weather is bad or you can't leave the house, this indoor program presents the best alternative.

■ **Indoor Walking on the Treadmill** (page 99). The tips for indoor walking on the treadmill are for the beginning, advanced, and power walkers.

They will enable people to visit a health club and design the optimal exercise program for themselves, or do so at home on their own treadmill.

Use the walking test (page 46) to find the program that is right for you. As you continue your walking training, changes in your level of fitness and health will always occur. The increase in the level of fitness is always more noticeable in beginners than it is in the more advanced power walkers. Regardless of the difference in the level of fitness, the following advice is relevant:

Exercise in moderation; start slowly and increase carefully. Pay attention to warning signals your body sends you. Respect your limits! (see page 41).

The Walking Programs

The eight different walking programs that follow can be adapted and adjusted to your needs. Your walking program should correspond to the state of your health and endurance level. Do a warm-up of simple loosening up, stretching, and strengthening exercises before every walk. If you know the state of your fitness, you know whether you are a beginning, advanced, or expert walker, and you can increase your fitness level optimally with a 12-week exercise program. At any rate, don't forget that having fun, dissolving physical tension and tiredness, relaxing, and increasing your sense of well-being are the main goals of walking.

Exercises for Feeling Good and Having Fun

Always keep foremost in your mind the old saying, "Everyone makes his own luck." Include something every day that is fun, that you love doing, that brings you beauty and joy, that gives you a sense of well-being. Look at the events of the day with serenity. And if the day becomes stressful, plan to have a moment of quiet and relaxation. The best and fastest way to relieve stress that has accumulated during the day is with an evening walk.

Allow enough time for walking. When time is limited, squeezing a walk between two appointments might backfire on you and result in more stress. The gentle exertion during a walk will relax you. Stale air from the office is quickly discharged when you can breathe fresh air; your lungs will welcome air rich in oxygen. Organs are washed in it. Your nervous system gets a pleasing massage. Blood vessels, constricted due to tension

Don't walk when pressed for time

during the day, have a chance to relax and expand, and all organs, having worked hard all day, are given a chance to recuperate in a gentle way. A comfortable warmth spreads throughout your system; thoughts tangled up in the problems of the day seem to vanish. You leave your everyday stress behind and gather new strength. Let your spirits soar. What sport other than walking can offer you all this?

Warming Up Body and Mind

Your body is with you for life. It is the base, the ultimate resource, the spring from which we gather strength and power.
• When you ask your body to work harder, you must warm up, otherwise the chances of premature wear and tear are great. Therefore, start every walking session slowly and warm up.

Don't forget the warm-up

■ Warming up begins in the mind: prepare mentally for the walk you are about to embark on. Collect your thoughts and concentrate on the warm-up exercises. Do this before every exercise so that you get a feel for it.

A Little Warm-Up Time

A warm-up is not an annoying compulsory exercise; it really is a necessary preparation. Feel yourself doing the movements, how the important muscles and muscle groups are gently stretched and loosened up. You will notice during the warm-up exercises that after every effort there is relaxation.

Depending on their condition, function, and the degree of effort exerted, muscles have a tendency to shorten and to become tired. At first, the muscles become shorter and the movements of the joints are diminished. For that reason, the main emphasis during warm-up is on stretching.

Stretching

First, muscles need to be warmed up before any stretching exercise can be successful. That is only accomplished through rhythmical move-

ments and by walking at a slow tempo. The reasons:

• A muscle that has been warmed up is more flexible and stretches more easily. The chances of injury are greater if you stretch first and then walk fast immediately.
• During stretching, the fibers that make up the muscle are lengthened and the passive elements—tendons and ligaments—are stretched out. In the process, the muscles become more flexible and move more easily. Ligaments and tendons, connecting the muscles and the bones and transferring muscle energy to the bones, adjust to regular

Warm up before you start to walk

stretching and become more pliable.

• Simple, regular stretching exercises help prevent injuries like muscle sprains. Over the long term, the mobility of the joints remains intact or improves.

Movement and coordina-tion

Coordination, the interplay of the muscles, also gets better when you warm up. The speed of nerve impulses that go from the brain to the muscles also increases when the body has been warmed up. More muscle groups are activated and the steps you take later while walk-ing are easier.

■ This is how you stretch your muscles:

• Slowly ease into the stretch. Don't hold your breath; breathe slowly and deeply. Quietly continue to breathe.

• Stretch your muscles slowly until you feel a comfortable sensation. Avoid abrupt or whipping movements.

• Stretch your muscles for 10 to 12 seconds, and then release slowly.

• Actively loosen your muscles by careful shaking, or use your hands and stroke and pat your muscles gently.

• Do the exercises twice on each side.

• Do the warm-up exercises in the sequence given.

Start every warm-up pro-gram by walking a few hun-dred meters, relaxed but at a good speed. This will stimulate circulation and the flow of blood to the muscles. The muscles will then stretch much more easily.

Walk a short distance before starting the warm-up

The Warm-Up Exercises

Leave time at the beginning of your walking session for your warm-up exercises. Do them in the sequence given here to avoid harmful stress. Pay attention to the important tips given. The warm-up exercises are equally effective for outdoor and indoor walking.

First Exercise: Pushing

Stretching the calf muscles

Look for an object—a tree, a wall, or some other solid support—that you can push against.

• Take a small step forward. Lean with both your arms against the tree. One leg remains stretched out behind you (see photo).

• Push your hips forward and down and push with your stretched-out arms against the tree, without losing the stretch of the leg behind you. Make sure that the whole foot is flat on the ground; do not lift the heel off.

• Do the exercise with the other leg extended. You have done the exercise correctly when you feel a mild stretch in the upper calf.

Keep the whole foot on the ground

Second Exercise: Bending

Stretching the calf muscles

For this exercise, find a tree, a wall, or some other solid object that will provide you with support.

• Slightly bend both knees (photo page 62).
• The hips push down slightly. The feet remain flat on the ground.
• Repeat the exercise with the other leg.

Pushing

Bending

Third Exercise:
Take a Bow

Stretching the backs of the thighs

For this exercise, find a park bench or an object on which you can rest one leg.
• Place one leg on the park bench, with knee straight. Put one hand flat on your chest; use the other as a support for the lower back (see photo).
• Lean your upper body forward until you feel your hand resting in the hollow of the lower back. With your other hand, feel how your chest expands under your hand. In this position, move the upper body towards the leg that is resting on the park bench. Stretch only to the point where you can feel a stretching sensation in the back of the thigh and the back of the knee.
• Repeat the exercise with the other leg.
   Important: the back must remain in the position described above.
• Check your hands, where you have placed them, to see if you are able to hold this position.
• As soon as your hand can't feel the hollow in the lower back, or the hand on your chest begins to move, don't stretch the muscles in the backs of the thighs anymore.
• Any movement of the upper body other than leaning forward is "cheating" and indicates that the lower spine is moving, which could stress the ligaments of the lumbar verte-

Take a bow

brae, which, in turn, could lead to premature wear and tear of the vertebrae.

Fourth Exercise: Forward Step

Stretching the hip muscles

• Take a step forward, somewhat further than you normally do (see photo). The back leg is straight, the front leg may be bent slightly.

• Stretch your upper body as you place your hands loosely on top of each other on the upper thigh of the leg in front. The upper body is an extension of the stretched-out back leg (see photo).

Upper body and back leg are in one line

• Now, move the upper body slightly back, without changing your posture. Your hands will feel the change.

• Repeat the exercise with the other leg.

The exercise is done correctly when you feel the stretch in the pelvic area and the inside of the thighs.

Forward step

Fifth Exercise: The Crane

Stretching the muscles in the fronts of the thighs

• Stand upright. Tighten your stomach and buttock muscles to avoid hollowing your back. Tightening these muscles allows the back to remain fixed and the muscles in the front of the thigh to be stretched without the participation of any other muscle groups and without creating unnecessary stretching of the lower back.

The crane

The side step

• Bend your leg and pull your foot with one hand. If you find it difficult to keep your balance, use the free hand to support yourself on any solid surface.

• Pull the heel of the foot that you are holding slowly toward your buttocks (left photo), until you can feel the front muscles of your thigh begin to stretch. Pull your hips slightly forward to prevent hollowing your back.

• Repeat the exercise with the other leg.

Sixth Exercise:
Side Step

Stretches for the sides of the thighs

• Take one step to the side. The upper body remains upright. The feet face straight ahead (right photo).

• Shift your weight to one leg, meanwhile slightly bending the knee, but not beyond a right angle. The opposite leg remains straight.

• Repeat the exercise on the other side.

Wave the
flag

The
butterfly

Seventh Exercise: Wave the Flag

Stretching the muscles at the side of the torso, and mobilizing the lumbar spine

• Stand upright on both feet, with your feet slightly apart. Both arms lie relaxed alongside the side seam of your pants.
• Lift the left arm above your head and bend to the right. The right arm moves down at the same time. Move the left arm over to the right side (left photo).
• Repeat the exercise on the other side.
   Note: Do not bend forward with the upper body

Eighth Exercise: The Butterfly

Stretching the chest muscles

You need a tree for support.
• Stand next to a tree that is big enough to push against. Position yourself near it. Place one arm on the trunk, slightly above shoulder height, and lean against the trunk of the tree (right photo).
• Turn the upper body opposite the stretched-out arm until you can feel the stretch in the chest muscles. Don't hollow your back; support your back by tightening your stomach and buttock muscles.
• Repeat the exercise with the other arm extended.

Neck
stretch

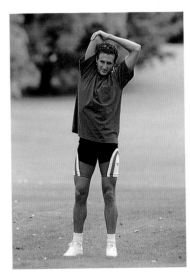

Elbow pull

Ninth Exercise:
Neck Stretch

**Stretching the muscles on
the side of the neck**

Stand relaxed but upright. Put
your feet about a shoulder-
width apart. Look straight
ahead.
• With the right hand, reach
over the top of your head
toward your left ear.
• Move your head slightly to
the right side (left photo).
• Move the left shoulder down
in the direction of the floor
until you can feel the muscles
of the neck stretch out.
• Repeat the exercise with the
other side.

Tenth Exercise:
Elbow Pull

**Stretching the upper arm
muscles**

• Stand upright, with your feet
shoulder-width apart. Bend
your right arm over your head
towards your back (see photo).
• With your left hand, reach
over your head and grab your
elbow.
• With your left hand, pull the
bent right arm in the direction
of your left shoulder.
• Repeat the exercise, switch-
ing arms.

The 10 Warm-Up Exercises

Exercise	Muscles Affected
1. Pushing	Small and large calf muscles
2. Bending	Calf muscles
3. Take a Bow	Back of thigh and calf muscles
4. Forward Step	Hip muscles
5. Crane	Front of thigh muscles
6. Side Step	Thigh muscles
7. Wave the Flag	Torso muscles, lumbar spine
8. Butterfly	Chest muscles
9. Neck Stretch	Side of neck muscles
10. Elbow Pull	Upper arm muscles

Do each exercise twice on each side of the body.

Quick Relief for Back Pain

If you sometimes feel stiff or suffer from occasional back pain, consider adding these exercises to your walking program; they are designed specifically to strengthen your back.

The exercises recommended here are for strengthening and stretching each group of muscles. Muscles that lack strength, or whose ability to stretch is diminished, may cause back pain.

Already-existing back problems can get worse unless you include some additional exercises for your back. Stomach and back muscles are often weakened due to lack of movement and uneven loads; this happens to most of us to a greater or lesser degree. Muscle imbalance is the reason for many difficulties in this part of the body. When an imbalance of the back muscles exists, the lumbar spine is not adequately supported above the hips.

Most often, the muscles of the fronts and backs of the thighs, the hips, and the back tend to contract. This situation, combined with weak stomach muscles, changes the posture and leads to muscle tightness or undue stress on the tendons and ligaments of the spine.

The following exercises are for all those who in their daily activities suffer from back pain. If you have had chronic back pain of longer duration, see your physician and show him or her the exercises we are recommending before beginning. Also, refer to the chapter on warm-up exercises. There you will find general advice about exercising.

Hip and Lower Back Exercises

To help the hips and lower back, the following muscle groups need stretching:

• Calf muscles (see Pushing, page 61)

Back, stomach, and buttock muscles

- Front and back thigh muscles (see Take a Bow and The Crane, pages 62 and 63)
- Hip muscles (see Forward Step, page 63, and Kneeling Step on this page)
- Back muscles (see Wave the Flag, page 65)

You need to strengthen the following:

- Stomach muscles (see Crunch, page 70)
- Buttock muscles (see Four-footed Stand, Hip Stretch, page 71)

Stretching calf, front and back thigh muscles, and the muscles for bending your hips is discussed in the warm-up exercise chapter (see page 60). What follow here are exercises for stretching your back muscles and strengthening the muscles in your stomach and buttocks.

Exercises for the Hips and Lower Back

First Exercise:
Take a Bow

Stretching the upper thigh muscles and the calf muscles; see page 62

Kneeling step

Second Exercise:
Kneeling Step

Stretching the front of thigh muscles and the hip flexors

- Take a big step forward. Kneel with the back leg on the ground (see photo). The knee angle should be at least 90°.
- With the upper body upright, push your hips forward, stabilizing the hips by tightening the stomach and buttock muscles. Can you feel the stretching sensation in the lower back area?

**Rocking
the back**

Crunch

*Third Exercise:
Rocking the Back*

**Stretching the back
muscles**

- Lie on your back.
- Fold both legs up and hold
them behind the knees with
both arms (left photo). By
slightly bending and stretching your knees, you will create
a gentle rocking motion;
make sure that you head does
not touch the floor!
- Rock back and forth for
about 30 seconds and feel the
muscles relaxing and the mas-
sagelike sensation.

*Fourth Exercise:
Crunch*

**Strengthening the stomach
muscles**

- Lie on your back.
- Place your heels and lower
legs on a chair as shown.
Raise your head first, then the
shoulders, then the upper
back (right photo).
- Hold this position for 10
seconds.
- Repeat this exercise 10
times.

Four-footed stand

Hip stretch

Fifth Exercise: Four-Footed Stand

Strengthening the back muscles

- Go down on all fours.
- First, stretch the right arm ahead of you; then push the left leg straight back (left photo).
- Hold this position for 10 seconds.
- Then pull the knee and leg forward and the arm back below the body; the hand touches the knee.
- Repeat this exercise 10 times on each side.

Sixth Exercise: Hip Stretch

Strengthening the buttock muscles

- Lie down on your back.
- Bend your knees as shown so your spine is straight. Lift your seat off the floor until you feel the muscles in the hip area stretching (right photo).
- Pay attention to the tension in your buttock muscles.
- Hold the tension for 10 seconds.
- Repeat the exercise 5 times.

Shoulders and Upper Back

Muscles in the upper part of the body and shoulder area are particularly vulnerable to lack of movement and uneven daily loads on one side. They quickly lose their strength. Neck muscles and muscles in the fronts of the shoulders, as well as the chest muscles, become less flexible and start to shorten. The result is a bad posture, which causes tightness and overworked tendons and ligaments. It is particularly important to strengthen and stretch the muscles in the area of the shoulders and neck vertebrae.

You will be stretching:

• Neck musculature
• Chest musculature

You will be strengthening:

• Muscles that support the back

Show your physician the exercises

If you suffer from either acute or chronic problems in this part of your body, check with your physician and show him or her the exercises you plan to do. When you do the strengthening exercises, do them slowly.

Exercises for the Shoulders and Upper Back

First Exercise:
Reaching and Stretching

Activating muscles used for stretching the back

• Alternately stretch your arms above your head as far as you can; stand on your toes (see photo). Can you feel the muscles on the sides of your body stretching?
• Continue this exercise for 30 seconds.

Reaching and stretching

Arm stretches

Head-turning

Second Exercise:
Arm Stretches

Stretching the chest muscles; strengthening the back muscles

• Raise both stretched-out arms to shoulder height and stretch them as far back and up as you can (left photo).
• Try to hold this position for 8 to 10 seconds.
• Repeat the exercise 3 to 5 times.

Third Exercise:
Head-Turning

Mobilizing neck vertebrae

• Slowly turn your head to the left and then to the right as far as you can (see photo). Inhale and exhale consciously during the exercise, with your eyes following your head movement.
• Hold the end position for 3 to 5 seconds on each side.
• Repeat each exercise 10 times on each side.

Fourth Exercise:
Neck Stretch

Stretching side and back muscles of the neck. For instructions, see page 66.

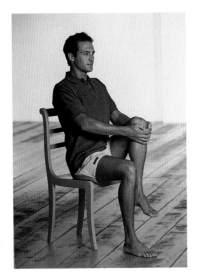

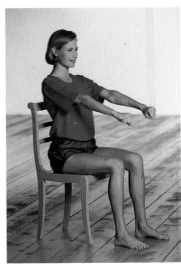

Total body tension

Arm tension

Fifth Exercise:
Total Body Tension

**Strengthening the muscles
of the shoulder blades**

• Sit upright in a chair. Raise
one leg high and hold the knee
with both hands interlaced.
• Pull your shoulders back.
Try to push the leg down
against the resistance created
by your hands (left photo).
• Hold this position for 10
seconds.
• Repeat this exercise 5 times
with each leg.
• Make sure you consciously
tighten the shoulder and buttock muscles.

Sixth Exercise:
Arm Tension

**Strengthening and
relaxing the arms**

• Sit upright in a chair. Raise
both arms, making fists (right
photo), and tighten every muscle in the arms and shoulders
for about 10 seconds. Breathe
quietly and rhythmically.
• Close your eyes and let your
arms hang down. Concentrate
of the feeling of warmth.
Enjoy the sensation of the
warmth as it moves from the
tips of your fingers through
the arms.
• Repeat the exercise 3 times.

Overview of Back Exercises

Exercises for Hips and Lower Back

Exercise	Effect on the Muscles Used
1. Take a Bow	Stretches back of thigh muscles and calf muscles
2. Kneeling Step	Stretches front of thigh muscles and hip flexors
3. Rocking the Back	Stretches back muscles
4. Crunch	Strengthens stomach muscles
5. Four-Footed Stand	Strengthens back extensor muscles
6. Hip Stretch	Strengthens buttock muscles

Exercises for Shoulders and Upper Back

1. Reaching and Stretching	Activates back extensor muscles
2. Arm Stretches	Stretches chest and back muscles
3. Head-Turning	Mobilizes neck vertebrae
4. Neck Stretch	Stretches the side and back muscles of the neck
5. Total Body Tension	Strengthens the shoulder blade muscles
6. Arm Tension	Strengthens and relaxes arms

Basic Walking Programs

The following walking programs have been designed to go with the results of the walking test. This lets you choose the walking program that corresponds to your present condition and age. The tables with each program list the optimum heart rate, duration of each individual exercise session, and how often you should walk every week.

	Max.	Exercise Heart Rates			
Age	100%* 60%	75%	80%	90%	
20	200	120	150	160	180
25	195	117	146	156	176
30	190	114	143	152	171
35	185	111	139	148	167
40	180	108	135	144	162
45	175	105	131	140	158
50	170	102	128	136	153
55	165	99	124	132	149
60	160	96	120	128	144
65	155	93	116	124	140
70	150	90	113	120	135

Exercise Heart Rates* for 20- to 70-Year-Olds

*Heart rates are given in beats/minute. Maximum heart rate (100%) is 220 minus your age. For example: 220–20 = 200 beats/minute, the estimated maximum heart rate for a person aged 20. Exercise heart rates are based on a percentage of the maximum heart rate for your age group.

Testing the Waters: for Beginners

For test result D

This is the perfect walking program if the result of your test is D. Your present level of endurance will quickly improve through gentle walking. The target heart rate listed in the program overview has taken into consideration your below-average performance on the walking test and the fact that you first have to get used to the effort that walking will require. Do not forget to warm up every time before you are to walk (see page 59).

Always pay attention to the signs from your body, such as being out of breath or feeling discomfort in the chest. If you notice these symptoms, stop, go back home, and make an appointment to see your physician.

Weeks 1 through 8

In the first 8 weeks, work up to achieving 60% of maximum heart rate during your walk. The slow increase will give your heart and circulatory system time to adjust to the extra stress load. Tendons and ligaments will be able to stretch gently. Look at the table of exercise heart rates (page 76) for the line that corresponds to your age. Walking 15 to 30 minutes once a week guarantees that you will not overtax your system and in the process spoil your newfound activity. Keep an eye on your walking technique.

Gently ease into the exercises

Overview: Testing the Waters: for Beginners

Week	1–8	9–16	17–24	25–32	33
Exercise heart rate* (% of max. heart rate)	60%	60%	75%	80%	Walking test
Duration of each session (in minutes)	15–30	30–45	45–60	60	Walking test
Sessions per week	1	2	2–3	3–4	Walking test

Weeks 9 through 16

These next eight weeks are designed to solidify what you have accomplished so far. First increase the duration of each walk to 30 to 45 minutes. Maintain the heart rate of weeks 1 through 8. Until the 12th week, walk about twice a week.

What you have done so far is already quite an accomplishment, even if you do not increase your tempo. That speed increase will come in the following week.

Do not increase speed

Weeks 17 through 24

During these eight weeks, increase the speed to a point where your heart rate reaches about 75% of your maximum heart rate (see the heart rate table on page 76). This corresponds to the lower range of the physical stress load that sports medicine doctors have recommended for endurance sports. In this phase you are, in any case, at the optimum ratio between oxygen intake and consumption (see information on the steady state, page 34). This guarantees that your system is not overtaxed. Towards the end of this phase, increase your walking sessions to three times a week.

Weeks 25 through 32

Increase your weekly walking seesions to 4 times a week and extend each session to 60 minutes per session until you have reached 80% of your maximum heart rate. In this way, you are improving your endurance level in a very gentle and safe manner. For some time now, you will have noticed some physical improvements: your resting pulse may be lower or perhaps you can now walk faster without increasing your heart rate.

Week 33

Now is the time for another walking test. You will most certainly realize that your physical condition has improved and that you can walk faster without becoming tired.

Increased fitness alone should be motivation enough for you to continue. Find out if you are can now move on to the advanced walking program. Continued increase in your fitness level has already been preprogrammed.

Increasing your fitness motivates you

Walking Program for Advanced Walkers

Walking test results B or C

The advanced walking program is useful for people at several performance levels. If the result of your walking test falls between B and C, the advanced program is for you.

Weeks 1 through 8

Train twice a week. At the end of the seventh week your training heart rate should reach 75% of your maximum heart rate (see the Heart Rate table on page 76 for reference). Try to walk at this tempo for about 45 minutes per session.

Fine-tune and perfect your technique during this period. In this way you are solidifying, and in the next phase will be able to increase the endurance level that the walking test has established.

Weeks 9 through 16

In this phase you should increase the length of each walk and the number of times you walk each week. Walk fast enough so that you can reach 75% of your maximum heart rate.

Weeks 17 through 24

Walk 4 times a week

Again, increase the length of time you walk. First, increase it to 60 minutes and then increase the sessions to 4 times a week. The walking intensity should be such that your heart rate is always at the lower end of the 75% exercise heart rate.

Overview of Program for Advanced Walkers

Week	1–8	9–16	17–24	25–32	33
Exercise heart rate* (% of max. heart rate)	60–75%	60–75%	75%	80%	Walking test
Duration of each session (in minutes)	30–45	45	45–60	60	Walking test
Sessions per week	2	3	3–4	4	Walking test

*See page 76 for table of heart rates for your age group.

Weeks 25 through 32

Now increase the level of your fitness and endurance by increasing your walking speed. Monitor your heart rate so that you do not go too fast; 80% of your maximum heart rate is quite sufficient.

Week 33

At the start of the 33rd week, take the walking test to see if your fitness level has increased. Since you can expect this to be the case, and since your endurance is most likely at an excellent level, you might want to think about advancing to the power-walking program. This program is the most likely way to further increase and improve the level of your fitness.

Power Walking for the Ambitious

If your walking test result is A

Power walking is the highest level of achievement in walking and is for the very ambitious and well-trained walker.

If your walking test result was A (see page 52), power walking is the right program for you. Here, too, the guideline is: "Start gently and increase slowly." In this program, you should become familiar with the walking tech-

nique during the first 8 weeks.

Weeks 1 through 8

During this phase, don't walk as fast as you probably could. It is better to wait until your system has adjusted to the gentle increase in intensity that is to follow. Your endurance is good, but tendons and ligaments need time to adjust. Make use of a medium walking speed to fine-tune your technique, because the technique must be correct in order for you to walk at the maximum tempo.

Always keep an eye on your technique

Weeks 9 through 16

In this phase, you increase the length of each walk without reaching the 80% heart rate level. (That will happen from the 17th week on, when you try to walk for 90 minutes for each outing at the 75%–80% endurance fitness level.) Increase the number of outings to 3 or 4 per week.

Weeks 17 through 24

Increase to 90 minutes power walking at almost maximum speed (75–80% of maximum heart rate). You are so fit, you think you could uproot a tree. But it will get even better.

Weeks 25 through 32

You can now move into walk-

Walk for up to 2 hours ing to achieve 90% of your maximum heart rate. This will increase your endurance fitness still further. You can increase the sessions per week from 4 to 7, and the session length from 90 to 120 minutes.

Week 33

Take another walking test (see page 46) to see if there is still more room for improvement, such as increasing your speed and improving your test heart rate. If after the initial test you can walk faster with a lower heart rate, your endurance fitness capability has reached the top and most likely can't be improved upon.

You can increase the training intensity by wearing weights on your wrists, which will also make your chest and shoulder muscles work harder. The more muscle groups you activate, the more efficient the use of your physical resources and, in turn, the greater the effect. Always include rest periods between your walks because regeneration and exercise load need to be in balance. Furthermore, don't walk on a regular basis beyond the 80% maximum heart rate limit. The 90% mentioned above is only meant to add new stimulation to your system in order to reach a higher adaptation effect.

Don't forget to have rest periods

Overview of Power Walking for the Ambitious

Week	1–8	9–16	17–24	25–32	33
Exercise heart rate* (% of max. heart rate)	60–75%	75%	75–80%	90%	Walking test
Duration of each session (in minutes)	30–45	45–60	60–90	90–120	Walking test
Sessions per week	2–3	3–4	4	4–7	Walking test

*See page 76 for table of heart rates for your age group.

Special Walking Programs

Walking as described in this book can do more than just improve your health. In this section, we give specific programs for specific people: body-conscious walking, where you learn how to achieve peace physically and mentally; the walking program for older people, where you learn how to remain fit physically and mentally for many years (page 85); and the walking program for weight loss, which will help you to shed those extra pounds in a pleasant way (page 87).

Relaxing with Body-Conscious Walking

Unity of body and mind

The development of the mind begins with bodily experiences. Physical exercises influence mental development. In this sense, body-conscious walking is for all those who want to reach their mind via the body and who also want to learn about themselves through meditation and relaxation.

The movements during body-conscious walking are rhythmic and harmonious; they don't have a beginning or end. Everything flows into and out of everything else. Body-conscious walking gives you a sense of physical and spiritual unity.

Life energy flows into your body with each breath and is the guide for your body's movements while you walk. Your body is the medium through which you experience and look at the world around you in a new way. It is important that you find your rhythm, the walking tempo that is right for you. The effects of body-conscious walking are achieved by paying careful attention to your body.

Become aware of your breathing

■ Find a place for your walk that is free of commotion, noises, and traffic. Concentrate in order to prepare yourself for each walk.
• To do that, stand quietly and focus your attention. Let the weight of your body sink down into your feet, anchoring you solidly to the ground. Earth's strength is permeating your body. Now, do the warm-up exercises (page 61). Begin to think yourself into

body-conscious walking by imagining gentle, flowing and harmonious walking movements.

• Slowly start to walk. Your posture is upright and comfortable, your body relaxed. You feel light and mobile. Your mind is quiet. All you do is concentrate on your walk. Increase your speed to a medium, comfortable level.

• Body-conscious walking is closely related to your breathing—the way the air flows into your body as you inhale and exhale, reaching every part of your body. You are opening up and are cleansing your interior. Each breath will naturally become deeper.

Releasing tension

• Breathing enables you to release the tension in your muscles. Breathe into the part of the body that is tense. Breathe "into the arm" or "into the stomach." Feel how new energies are freed up, how energy blockages dissolve, and how life's energy begins flowing unhindered through your body.

• The walking movements and your mind become one. You walk relaxed and free of tension. The walking movement originates in the center of your body. The center of the body, your hips and pelvis, is your foundation. Leg and arm motions are relaxed, continuous, and harmonious.

• Concentrate on this rhythmical movement. Feel how a comfortable heaviness is spreading through your body. The heaviness is sinking into your feet. You feel as if new strength is flowing into your body from there. If weather and the ground allow it, walk barefoot. Soft but firm sand or the springiness of the forest floor are ideal.

• Slowly you become one with the environment. Your senses are wide open to your inner and outer world. With every breath, you are taking in the environment, you can feel it in every fiber of your being. Allow these impressions to envelop you.

You feel the wholeness and unity of everything that surrounds you; you begin to feel being a small part of the universal whole. You know that you are connected and part of everything that is surrounding you. An undreamed-of sense of security and relaxation spreads through your body. You feel like a drop of water flowing in the safety of the river of life. Past, present, and future become one. You are living in the here and now and are carried by the motion of your body-conscious walking.

Experience yourself as part of the whole

1: Body-conscious walking, withdrawal phase. Pull your fists up.

2: Body-conscious walking, withdrawa phase. Relax your limbs

• Cherish this sense of happiness. It is in these moments when you understand the world, your world as it reveals itself only to you. Body-conscious walking gives you a sensuous experience of the world as a whole.

• At the conclusion of your exercise, return from this experience of self-absorption actively. Always do the withdrawal exercise. It will bring you back relaxed, with a clear and quiet mind. Skip the withdrawal exercise only if you are going to bed immediately after your body-conscious walk.

Withdrawal exercise
Slowly decrease your walking tempo until you come to a standstill. Stand quietly and securely, the way you did at the beginning of the exercise. Let the heaviness of your body sink down into your feet. Make fists, tense all muscles in your arms, and pull your fists up to your chest vigorously several times (see photo 1). Inhale and exhale several times, audibly and deeply. Relax your limbs (see photo 2). Look around you, wide awake.

Try to do body-conscious walking as often as possible. Take your time while you do it. Getting used to paying attention to your body requires patience. You may not notice the effects immediately. What is important is that you walk regularly.

There are no particular instructions for how long you should do body-conscious walking. Inexperienced walkers may need more time in the beginning to reach a meditative and relaxed state than those who are more experienced. Paying attention to your breathing and getting a sense of the rhythmical movement of walking are more important during body-conscious walking than watching your speed and pulse rate.

Concentration and withdrawal exercises

Take your time with body-conscious walking, concentration, and the withdrawal exercise. They are all important components in the practice of centering and of focusing life's energies that reside within your body.

A tip for nature lovers: body-conscious walking is particularly beautiful in the morning at sunrise or in the evening at sunset. Try to get a sense of how a sleeping world awakens to new life or how the turmoil of the day relaxes into peacefulness.

Walking Program for Older People

This walking program was specially designed for people age 70 and older. If you are in this age group, walking is the ideal endurance sport for you. Mobility, vitality, well-being, and health not only remain intact through regular walking, but are increased. The quality of life improves. You gain trust in the strength of your body. The goal: to be and remain fit and productive far into old age.

The ideal program for people over 70

Moderate walking keeps the heart and circulatory system in shape, provides the brain with a better blood flow, activates the metabolic processes, and keeps blood pressure under control. All muscles and bones are strengthened. The tendency to fall and get fractures is reduced through constant interaction between the nerves and muscles, which, in the process, remain healthy.

■ The time you need to spend walking is the same amount that you used for your daily, extended leisurely walk. Your goal is to walk daily for 45 to 60 minutes at 80% of your maximum heart rate.

Exercise Heart Rates for Older People

Age	Max. 100%*	Exercise Heart Rates 60%	75%	80%
70	150	90	113	120
75	145	87	109	116
80	140	84	105	112
85	135	81	101	108
90	130	78	97	104

*Maximum heart rate (220 minus age in years).

Your maximum heart rate = 200 minus your age.

Example: A person 80 years of age should walk to achieve a heart rate of approximately 112 beats per minute (80% of maximum; see table).

The values listed in the table are meant as a guide. What is important, regardless of the exercise phase you happen to be in, is that you never exceed your resting heart rate by more than 10 beats per minute. This

Overview of Walking for Older People

Week	1–8	9–16	17–24	25–32	33
Exercise heart rate* (% of max. heart rate)	60%	60%	75%	80%	80%
Duration of each session (in minutes)	15	15–30	30–45	45–60	45–60
Sessions per week	1	2	2–3	3–4	4–7

*See table above for heart rates for your age group.

means that if your pulse is 80 beats per minute when you are standing still, your walking pulse should be 90 beats per minute. This will give you the results you want without over-taxing your system.

Target heart rate is the bench-mark

The target heart rates given in the tables are only guides, because the level of fitness and state of health can vary greatly among older people. Some are still able to "uproot a tree," while other are "feeling their age." And anyhow, we are not talking about winning a medal, only about your own feeling of well-being.

Walking is even better when you can do it with friends or acquaintances. It just is more fun in a group. You can talk to each other, make contacts, and deepen friendships. Together you are strong—and no longer alone.

Slimming and Weight Loss Through Walking

Walking is an endurance sport that also helps you to burn your body's fat deposits. Walking is kind to your joints, and is the best endurance sport for people who want to lose weight or keep from gaining weight. Regular walking is

Reducing your "spare tire"

better than going on a diet. Walking changes the ratio of fat to muscle mass in a very positive way. A focused weight-reduction program can be supported by eating a diet of fewer calories (see pages 89–90).

Eat less

When you walk, your body uses energy in the form of car-bohydrates and fats that are stored in the body. Energy-producing substances in the muscles are used up at a higher rate, burning more food than when you diet.

Walk according to your age group and the corresponding exercise heart rates listed in the heart rate table (page 76). It is important that you walk 60 minutes each session, ideally, because it is then that 50–70% of your energy comes from burning body fats.

If you have high blood pres-sure or suffer from aching joints—two conditions that are often associated with being overweight—you should seek advice from your physician before starting this walking program.

Overview: Slimming and Weight Loss Through Walking

Week	1–8	9–16	17–24	25–32
Exercise heart rate* (% of max. heart rate)	60%	60%	75%	80%
Duration of each session (in minutes)	15	15–30	45	60
Sessions per week	4	4	5	7

*See table on page 76 for heart rates for your age group.

Weeks 1 through 8

During the first 8 weeks of the program, start slowly. Give hip, knee, and foot joints time to adjust to the stress. We suggest that you walk about 4 times a week for 15 minutes each. Combine the program with a calorie-reducing diet.

Walk 4 times a week for ½ hour

Weeks 9 to 16

For the next 8 weeks, increase your walking to 30 minutes per walk, 4 times a week. This will cause the fat to start being metabolized. Continue eating low-calorie foods.

Weeks 17 through 24

Now increase your walking to 5 times per week, 45 minutes per session. Your body will only be able to do this by drawing on its fat reserves. During this phase you will most likely be losing weight, or you will notice that your skin is tightening and parts of your body—the buttocks, stomach, and legs—are becoming more shapely.

Walk vigorously for an hour every day

Weeks 25 to 32

Now you are going full tilt. Walk 60 minutes every day, which means using and burning body fat every day. This in turn means losing weight.

Walking and Food

All foods consist of the following components:

- Carbohydrates
- Fats
- Proteins

Vitamins and minerals

In addition to these 3 main components, food further contains vitamins and minerals that are essential for life. Vitamins perform several tasks in the metabolic process and in the uptake of nutrients. For that reason, make sure that you are getting sufficient amounts of these nutritional substances. When you walk, your system loses salt and minerals. Salt is essential for your body's water needs. Your body's cells play a role in the digestion of the food you eat, transforming the dissolved substances directly into energy or storing them as a reserve for times between meals.

Normally, your body burns all the carbohydrates and fats that it gets from the food you eat. Proteins do not provide energy directly, but aid in metabolic and digestive processes. Food high in fats and sugars can cause imbalances in these processes. Improper food, together with lack of exercise, greatly increases the chances for weight gain. Of course, our bodies are able to compensate for these factors, but only for so long. Sooner or later this balancing act is exhausted.

Make sure, therefore, that the food you eat is varied and contains the nutrients the body needs: two-thirds of the calories should come from grain products, potatoes, pasta, fruits, and vegetables and one-third should come from milk, yogurt, cheese, and lean meat.

Look for more information about properly balanced nutrition in books and magazines on the subject.

Six Tips for Good Nutrition

Balanced nutrition

Taking the following six tips into consideration will aid you to eat carefully and do so over time. Good nutrition will also increase your fitness level, because easily digestible food provides more energy for your body and makes you feel better.

1. Avoid fats and foods with high fat content.

2. Do not eat sugar and sweets. Sugar causes the blood sugar level to increase suddenly. In order to make up for this

sudden increase, the pancreas must produce and quickly pour a great deal of insulin into the bloodstream. This creates on one hand more work for the pancreas. On the other hand, a sudden increase in insulin also makes you feel hungry very quickly, although the body has sufficient energy available, because the blood sugar level drops below its original level.

3. Drink fewer alcoholic beverages. Regular consumption of alcohol over a long period of time does damage to the liver, the nervous system, and the brain. It reduces coordination and reaction time. Alcohol after a walk reduces the level of blood sugar, which can lead to a collapse of the circulatory system. Recovery time after a walk takes longer.

4. Replace white flour with whole wheat products. White flour products lack the fiber that is present in those made from whole wheat. Fiber is contained in the outer hull of the wheat kernel, among other things. When fiber reaches the digestive tract, it is not digested, but expelled unchanged. Fiber stimulates the digestive system, takes up toxic substances, and the body stays satisfied (not hungry) longer.

5. Eat five small meals a day. Five meals a day provide your body and your digestive system with an even load. Blood sugar levels remains constant and at a proper level. This prevents the feeling of tiredness often experienced after eating a large meal.

6. Drink plenty of water. Drink at least 2 liters (2 quarts) a day; for example, mineral water, fruit juice, or tea. When you walk, increase the water intake to 4 liters (4 quarts) a day.

Walking During Convalescence

Walking can serve as therapy and restore and stabilize former fitness levels rather quickly. In certain cases, walking can be an excellent addition to traditional therapies for problems like osteoporosis (decrease in bone mass and density), injuries and wear on the tendons, muscles, and joints, and heart conditions.

Walking is therapy

The walking during convalescence program should only be done after close consultation with your physician and your physical therapist.

For Osteoporosis

Osteoporosis is a condition that for the most part afflicts women of middle age and up. Osteoporosis weakens the bones without altering their shape. At the end of the active growing phase (after the age of 35), an age-related process of decrease in bone mass and diminution begins. The condition is more severe in women than in men. The reason for it seems to be that the production of estrogen starts to decrease when women begin menopause. Signs of osteoporosis are back pain, particularly in the lower back, which is caused by small breakdowns of the vertebrae in that area.

Walking, combined with eating foods high in calcium, can help prevent osteoporosis. Calcium is important for the density and stability of bones and is present in milk products and meat, among other foods. Walking is good physical therapy for lessening the symptoms and even preventing osteoporosis when it is in the beginning stages; exercise walking is also very good because the impact on the joints is much less than that of other types of athletic activity.

Movement therapy

• If you have osteoporosis, ask your physician if you are allowed to walk. In the more advanced stages of the illness, only osteoporosis-specific exercises are allowed.

With Joint Injuries or Wear and Tear

Walking is also very good as physical exercise for people who suffer from problems resulting from foot, knee, and hip injuries and injuries to the back, who have to avoid the stress created by other types of exercise. Here, walking is better for regaining endurance and health than jogging or running.

During walking, the stress load is three times less than in running. For almost all types of injuries, walking can either maintain or, after a prolonged period of inactivity, reestablish the level of fitness you had before in a very short time.

Since the end of the 1960s, we have known that physical inactivity can lead to a worsening of a condition—for instance, in cases of arthrosis (joint damage). Sports medicine doctors have widely promoted moderate physical activity to either prevent an illness from worsening or at least stop its progression. Walking is one such moderate physical activity.

Heart monitor

With Heart Disease

Walking is also recommended as exercise for people with heart disease and is used for heart-specific endurance therapy. Here, walking as physical exercise is monitored and carried out under controlled conditions. Walking improves the metabolism of fat, increases the flow of blood (preventing deposits from settling inside the arteries), lowers blood pressure, and, through the action of the muscles, supports the return flow of the blood to the heart. For walking as a means of aftercare after a heart attack, a heart rate monitor is, in our opinion, an absolute must. For people involved in a heart-strengthening program, measuring devices that are as accurate as an EKG can also be used. Polar heart monitors fulfill this need. They weigh very little and serve as an early warning system for possible suddenly appearing complications.

■ If you have a heart condition, it is particularly important that you first get permission from your physician to make sure that you are allowed to walk.

Ask your physician

When the Weather Is Bad

An alternative to outdoor walking

When the weather won't cooperate, you can do your walking indoors at home or in a health club. It will reduce breaks in training that will surely affect your fitness level. Of course, walking is an outdoor sport that first and foremost is so effective because it takes place outside the house and in fresh air. Therefore, walk indoors only when temperatures are extreme—above 87°F (30°C) or below 15°F (–10°C)—or when it is raining heavily. In snowy and icy conditions, make sure that you walk in shoes or boots that have soles with treads that grip well.

Use the indoor walking program as an alternative to walking outdoors and always do it at the usual time of day—perhaps in the evening for relaxation after the stress of the day. Indoor exercise programs are also great to do at the office. You might even be able to entice your colleagues to join you. That would not only improve your fitness, but also the atmosphere in your office and everybody's well-being.

The tips for walking indoors on a treadmill (see page 99) are for people who are members of health clubs or fitness enthusiasts who have the space for a treadmill at home.

Calf exercise, step 1

Calf exercise, step 2

Indoor Gymnastics Program

In addition to a good mood, you need a chair, a blanket, a handkerchief, and a tennis ball, or a ball whose surface is covered with raised bumps. Exercise barefoot, because the indoor program is also good for your feet. Depending on how quickly you do your exercises, the indoor exercise program offered here will take about 30 to 45 minutes.

First Exercise: For the Calf Muscles

• Stand behind the back of a chair, feet apart.
• Raise yourself up on both feet (1), starting at your heels and moving along the length of your soles until you are standing on the balls of your feet (2).
• Repeat 10 to 15 times. Pay attention to the tension in your body. Look ahead, not down at your feet.

Foot rotation

Grabbing

Second Exercise: Foot Rotation

• Stand behind the back of a chair, feet slightly apart. You do not necessarily have to hold onto the back of the chair.
• Set one foot on floor with the tips of the toes resting on the floor. Your body weight is shifted onto the other foot (left photo).
• Now move the foot 5 to 7 times in a circle, in both directions, making the circle as large as possible. Change feeet and repeat the same exercise with the other foot.

Third Exercise: Grabbing

• Stand next to a chair, parallel to the back, feet slightly apart.
• With your toes, reach for a handkerchief on the floor and try to lift it and place it in front of the other foot.
• Repeat the exercise 5 to 10 times with each foot.

Changing feet

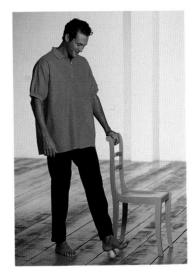

Foot massage

Fourth Exercise: Changing Feet

• Sit on the front edge of the chair. Your legs are stretched out in front of you, your upper body is upright. Support yourself with your arms (left photo).
• Flex and stretch your toes, alternately pointing each foot. Hold each end position for 4 to 6 seconds.
• Repeat this exercise 10 times.

Fifth Exercise: Foot Massage

• Stand behind a chair, feet slightly apart. Roll a tennis ball around on the floor with one foot (right photo). A ball covered with raised bumps is even better, because the bumps increase the effectiveness of the massage. Use the whole surface of the sole of your foot, from the heels across the ball of the foot and up to the toes. Repeat with the other foot.
• This exercise is particularly important for people who are on their feet a lot.
• Do this exercise for as long as you like, until you feel relaxed.

**Walking
in place**

**Stair
support**

*Sixth Exercise:
Walking in Place*

• Walk in place. One foot
must always be on the floor.
Arms assist with the movements, as in outdoor walking
(left photo).
•Of course, you cannot roll
your feet from the heels to the
toes, as you do in outdoor
walking. Try to raise your
knees with every step as high
as possible, but no more than
hip high.
• As in outdoor walking,
check your age-appropriate
heart rate. Walk for about 10
to 15 minutes.

*Seventh Exercise:
Stair Support*

• Last, but not least, give relief
to your back and feet. Lie
down on your back and place
your lower legs on the seat of a
chair (right photo). Relax! If
you like, you can read your
newspaper or a book. Do this
relaxation exercise for about 10
to 15 minutes.

Indoor Walking on the Treadmill

Walking in its truest form is really an outdoor sport. But sometimes you can't find anybody who will walk outside with you, or there may be no streets in your neighborhood suitable for walking. Perhaps you don't want to walk outside when the weather is bad, or you want to walk at night. If you face one of these situations, consider doing your walking on a treadmill: for fitness, for your figure, and for your health. This chapter discusses the specifics of walking on a treadmill and describes the advantages and disadvantages.

Walking Indoors, Whatever the Weather

Walking indoors is the ideal alternative to walking outdoors. One of the ways to do it is on the treadmill. Some treadmills are motor driven; some are not. The expensive motor-driven versions simulate normal walking. What is special about walking on a motor-driven treadmill is that the floor is moving under your feet. In contrast to walking on the street, where the length and frequency of each step and the speed of walking is determined by you, on the treadmill, you must adjust to the motion and speed of the treadmill's conveyor belt.

In the less expensive treadmills, which are not motor-driven, the conveyor belt (running belt) is moved by your muscle power. Entirely different criteria have to be considered for this type of walking than for walking on a motor-driven treadmill or normal outdoor walking. We discourage people from buying the cheaper versions of treadmills. The following tips are for using a modern, comfortable, motor-driven treadmill.

When treadmill walking, remember that it is very important to be loose and relaxed, otherwise you can easily lose the walking rhythm. Arm movements and breathing are the same as in outdoor walking; but forcefully pushing off with the toes should be eliminated because of the less-than-stable surface of the

Be loose and relaxed while walking on a treadmill

moving conveyor belt.

The correct shoes are very important
The correct shoes are very important when walking on a treadmill, because the surface is very hard. Read the discussion about The Right Shoes carefully. It is also best to wear light and comfortable clothing.

Why Use a Treadmill?

What is particularly attractive about indoor walking is that you are independent of the weather. Fresh air is what makes walking outside such a healthful activity, however; so make sure that enough fresh air is available when walking indoors, if possible.

Treadmills offer many different diagnostic possibilities and the optimal adjustments possible for any training program. By controlling speed and distance, it is easy to administer the 2 km walking test as well as the Conconi or the Cooper fitness test. Diagnostic measurements like the EKG, blood pressure, and lactate levels can easily be done because the person taking the test remains in one place. This is particularly important for patients under medical care.

The treadmill also has advantages when the training

level and stress load for power walking need to be adjusted, since it is easy to accurately regulate speed, angle of incline, and distance. With a device for measuring heart rate, it is possible to control the stress load, which is absolutely essential where walking is part of therapy. It is also useful for athletic training and for people who want to improve their general health. Modern treadmills are also very good for designing a

Many treadmills let you adjust the speed and incline to fit your needs

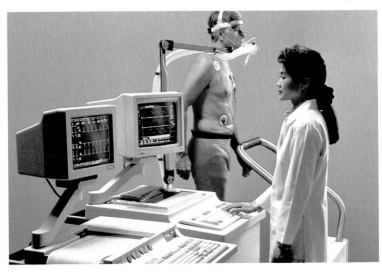

A treadmill with stress test system monitors cardiac activity during exercise. Shown with a multipurpose system that performs respiratory gas exchange measurements.

Below: A treadmill designed for cardiac rehabilitation or physical therapy

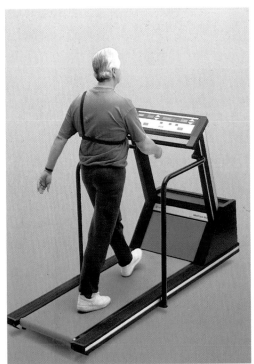

fitness program or to evaluate a stress profile.

Walking is ideal for communication. Because of the submaximal stress load, it is easy to have a conversation with a walking partner. This also holds true for indoor walking on the treadmill.

Walking on a treadmill is also ideal for people who want to be alone or who like some diversion. Music played in an exercise studio on a personal audiocassette player, or even a television can be used to add variety.

Such diversions can become dangerous, however. People who aren't experienced in walking on a treadmill risk injury because of the constantly moving running belt. Inattentiveness is punished swiftly by stumbling, tripping, or even a fall. Allowing for an adjustment period and keeping your concentration focused is the best prevention.

When on a treadmill, focus your concentration

What to Look for in a Treadmill

Treadmills should have certain basic features. Their presence indicates the quality of the equipment. Since manufacturers put new models on the market all the time, we have not listed any brand names, but only things that are found generally.

Generally speaking, treadmills should be easy to use and should have all the necessary training-specific features. Those features should include accurate speed control. The speed should be easy to read and easy to adjust. One particular advantage of the treadmill,

---

Desirable Treadmill Features

Equipment: Can be either motor driven or manually driven

Running-belt speed: Easily readable and adjustable in small increments

Angle of inclination: Adjustable from 0 to 15%

Training information: Distance, time interval, integrated heart rate measurements

Information about energy use: Calories used displayed

Safety features: *Length,* at least 58.5 inches (1.5 m). *Width,* at least 23 inches (.6 m). Has hand grips and an emergency shut-off

This tread-
mill is
compatible
with the
heart
monitor
the man is
wearing

in contrast to outdoor walking, is that the running belt can be raised at the front. This adjustment should also be easy to make, accurate, and clearly displayed. The angle of inclination of the conveyor belt should start at 0 and go to 15% in 1% increments. For training purposes, it is good if the treadmill is equipped with an integrated distance and time display.

Another feature, which is not absolutely necessary but is practical as a motivator (particularly for people who are trying to reduce their "spare tires"), is a display showing the calories used. Depending on the intensity, walking uses 300 to 500 calories per session.

An integrated heart rate monitor is particularly helpful for people with heart conditions, but it's also useful for those designing a general training program. The ideal treadmill also stores information about different stress-load profiles.

Last, there is the matter of safety. A treadmill should be equipped with adequate features for the hands to hold onto, as well as an emergency shut-off device. Both features are necessary in case you might stumble, to keep you from falling off the sides. A treadmill should also be wide and long enough for safe and comfortable use. The conveyor belt should at least 23 inches (.6 m) wide and 58.5 inches (1.5 m) long.

The display panel on some treadmills gives you feedback about heart rate, speed, calories burned, etc.

Is a Home Treadmill for You?

The models of treadmill that come with all the abovelisted features are expensive. They are usually found in fitness centers or health clubs. For home use, there are less expensive and simpler models. However, we discourage the purchase of a cheap treadmill. In any case, a treadmill costs more than a good bicycle or a bicycle ergometer. Before buying a treadmill for your home, you should consider:

• Do you have enough space in your home? Remember that a treadmill, unlike an ergometer, is more difficult to transport. A treadmill ought to be big enough so that you can have fun using it.

• Do you have a room with a sufficient amount of fresh air? Without fresh air, walking for health is far less effective.

• Are you familiar enough with treadmills to guarantee that you will really use it? If not, you might consider walking outdoors or join a fitness center or health club to learn about one first.

Indoor Walking Program for the Treadmill

The training guidelines are the same on the treadmill as for outdoor walking. You can therefore use the walking programs we have already discussed. However, you must find out which running belt speed is correct for you, so that you can exercise with the proper heart rate. But don't become a slave to the machine. Whether indoors or outdoors, walking should always be fun.

Beginning Walking on the Treadmill and Taking the Walking Test

If walking on a treadmill is new for you, take your time getting used to it. Start slowly until you are used to this unusual method of forward motion; then you can slowly increase your speed. Are you able to sustain a speed of at least 6 to 8 km (3.7 to 5 miles) per hour for 15 to 20 minutes? If you can breathe comfortably in the process, you can do the 2-km (1.2 mile) test: walk 2 km on the treadmill as fast as you can, and then measure your time and heart rate. Before you start, reread the section about the walking test. If you are not sure what to do, check with your physician or with the professionals at the health club.

Start slowly until you are used to the treadmill

What is the result of your test? Follow the instructions below for whichever group applies to you:

The result of my walking test is:
A B C D E

E. Discuss the state of your fitness with the professionals in the fitness center and your physician. You need advice before you start your walking program.

D. If the result is D, we recommend the beginner's program. Make sure that you take enough time to get used to walking on a treadmill before you try to walk at high speeds and for long time periods.

B, C. If your test result is B or C, we recommend the walking program for the advanced walker. You are already reasonably fit and can safely walk vigorously. But make sure that you feel comfortable and check your training pulse regularly.

A. You are a power walker, having finished the test with above-average results. For you, the treadmill is the best possible means of designing your training program. You can increase the angle of incline—walk uphill—and quickly notice how increasing the stresss load intensity also increases your training heart rate. The Power Walking for the Ambitious program is right for you.

*Men's Ideal Weights, by Height and Frame**

Height	Small	Medium	Large
5'2"	128–134	131–141	138–150
5'3"	130–136	133–143	140–153
5'4"	132–138	135–145	142–156
5'5"	134–140	137–148	144–160
5'6"	136–142	139–151	146–164
5'7"	138–145	142–154	149–168
5'8"	140–148	145–157	152–172
5'9"	142–151	148–160	155–176
5'10"	144–154	151–163	158–180
5'11"	146–157	154–166	161–184
6'	149–160	157–170	164–188
6'1"	152–164	160–174	168–192
6 2"	155–168	164–178	172–197
6'3"	158–172	167–182	176–202
6'4"	162–176	171–187	181–207

*Weight (in pounds) is measured in indoor clothing weighing 5 lbs for men (3 lbs for women) and shoes with 1-inch heels. Source: Build Study, 1979. Society of Actuaries and Associations of Life Insurance Medical Directors of America.

Women's Ideal Weights, by Height and Frame*

Height	Small	Medium	Large
4'10"	102–111	109–121	118–131
4'11"	103–113	111–123	120–134
5'	104–115	113–126	122–137
5'1"	106–118	115–129	125–140
5'2"	108–121	118–132	128–143
5'3"	111–124	121–135	131–147
5'4"	114–127	124–138	134–151
5'5"	117–130	127–141	137–155
5'6"	120–133	130–144	140–159
5'7"	123–136	133–147	143–163
5'8"	126–139	136–150	146–167
5'9"	129–142	139–153	149–170
5'10"	132–145	142–156	152–173
5'11"	135–148	145–159	155–176
6'	138–151	148–162	158–179

Source: Build Study, 1979. Society of Actuaries and Associations of Life Insurance Medical Directors of America.
*See notes on p. 108.

Acknowledgments and Photo Credits

Thanks to the Patagonia Company, Munich, Reebok Deutschland, Oberhaching, and Polar Electro GmbH Deutschland, Groß-Gerau, for lending us the clothing and props for the photos (pages 1–97). We thank Stefan Wachter for his assistance with the chapter on treadmill walking and for his constructive support.
Photos on pages 1–97 by Franz Faltermaier. Photos on cover as follows: Large front cover photo by Franz Faltermaier. Small front cover photo of ClubTrackPlus® commercial fitness treadmill courtesy of Quinton Fitness Equipment, Bothell, Washington.
Photos on pages 98–106 as follows: page 98 and 106: The M9.25 electronic treadmill from Precor has hand-rails and a computerized

tracking system that adjusts the motor and belt speeds. Photos courtesy of Precor® Incorporated, USA, Bothell, Washington.

page 100: The J660 electronic treadmill for home use from Tunturi® includes 5 preprogrammed workouts and can store information on the user's workout. Photo courtesy of Tunturi, Seattle, Washington.

page 101: The C944 commercial treadmill from Precor has a display showing user's workout in relation to target training zone; feedback adjusts belt speed. Photo courtesy of Precor® Incorporated, USA, Bothell, Washington.

page 102, top: The Q4500 Stress Test System monitors cardiac events during exercise. Shown with the QMC (Quinton Metabolic Cart), a multi-purpose system that performs respiratory gas exchange measurements. Photo courtesy of Quinton Instrument Company, Bothell, Washington.

page 102, bottom: MedTrack CR60, a rehabilitation treadmill, is designed for cardiac rehabilitation or physical therapy. Photo courtesy of Quinton Instrument Company, Bothell, Washington.

page 104: HR ClubTrack™, a commercial fitness treadmill, uses Polar®-compatible heart rate monitoring. Photo courtesy of Quinton Fitness Equipment, Bothell, Washington.

page 105, top: The M9.45 electronic treadmill from Precor has a running belt that can be inclined from -2 to 12% and includes computerized monitoring of your workout. Photo courtesy of Precor® Incorporated, USA, Bothell, Washington

page 105, bottom: The J550 electronic treadmill for home use from Tunturi® displays information on user's progress and is compatible with all Polar® pulse telemeters to provide instant heart-rate feedback. Photo courtesy of Tunturi®, Seattle Washington.

Index

advanced walkers' program, 43, 53, 54, 79–80
aerobic sport, 34
age, and walking test times: men, 48; women, 49
angina pectoris, 21
arm exercises, 66, 73, 74, 75, 84
arms and hands, position of, 45–46
arm stretches (exercise), 73
arm tension (exercise), 74
back: exercises, 63, 68–75; pain, 68
ball, rolled with foot (exercise), 96
barefoot walking, 30
beginners' walking, 53, 77–78
bending exercise, 61
blood pressure, 92
body-conscious walking, 82–85
body signals, 39, 41
bones, ligaments, 17, 40, 91
breathing, 19, 21, 25, 34–37, 82, 83
buttock muscles, exercises for, 71, 75
calcium, 91
calf muscles, 61, 69, 94
calories used, 104
check-up, physician's, 22
chest and shoulder muscles, 65, 72–74, 81
circulation, blood, 17, 21
clothing, 27
colds or fever, 41
convalescence, and walking, 55, 91–93
coordination, 60
correct walking technique, 43–44
crane (exercise), 63
crunch (exercise), 70
depression, 13
doctor. See physician
duration of walking test (charts), 39–40
elbow pull (exercise), 66
endurance, 43
exhaling, 36
fat, 19, 90, 92
fever, 20
fitness, 43, 55
food, 89–90
foot: exercises, 95–96; motion in walking, 28, 44, 100

forward step (exercise), 63
four-footed stand (exercise), 69
frequency of walking, 39–40. See also how often and how long to walk
gasping, 19, 35
grabbing (exercise), 95
gymnastics program, 94–97
hands, 45, 46
head-turning exercises, 73
heart: effects of walking, 17, 40, 85, 92; function of, 37, 50
heart disease, 22, 92
heart monitor, 92, 104
heart rate: how and where to measure, 38–39, 50–51; older people's, 86; resting, 21; training heart rate (ages 20–70), 38, 76; and walking speed, 37; and walking test, 50, 52–53, 101
heat, 29, 42
height and weight chart, 109
high blood pressure, 21
hiking, 22
hips and lower back, 63, 68–71, 75
hip stretch (exercise), 71
how often and how long to walk, 33; 39–40; beginners, 77; advanced, 79; power-walking, 80–81; body-conscious walking, 85; older people, 86; for slimming or weight loss, 88
ice pack, 42
indoor gymnastics program, 94–97
indoor walking, 55, 99–107
jogging, 22, 23
joint pain or injury, 20, 21, 28, 41, 42, 59, 92
joints and ligaments, 28, 59
kneeling step (exercise), 69
limits, knowing, 41
men: heart rates, 38; muscle mass, 50; walking test evaluation, 48
motivation, 32
muscle: effect on, 17; imbalances of, 68; mass, 50, 87; pain, 41, 42; and warm-up, 59
music, 31–32, 102
nature, 14, 29
neck, 66, 72, 73
nerve impulses, 60

nutrition, 89–90
older people (age 70 and up): exercise heart rates for, 86; walking program for, 85–87; and walking test, 46
osteoporosis, 91–92
overtraining, 41, 42
oxygen use during exercise, 17, 19, 34, 35, 36, 50, 58
ozone, 29
pain, 20, 21, 28, 36, 41, 42, 68, 72, 92
physician, consulting: for back exercises, 72; before starting to walk, 22; when choosing shoes, 28; before walking for weight loss, 87; before walking with osteoporosis, 91
planning time, 32, 33
Polar® heart monitors, 92
posture, 45
power walking: 53, 54; 80–81
pulse. See heart rate
pushing (exercise), 61
reaching and stretching (exercise), 72
relaxation, 82, 83
respiratory infection, 20
resting between outings, 39, 40, 42
risk-assessment before walking, 20
rocking the back (exercise), 70
routine, 33–34
sand, 30
shoes, 28, 100
shoulders and upper back, 45, 72–75
side pain, 36
side step (exercise), 64
slimming and weight loss, 19, 21, 87–89, 104
special walking programs (overview), 54–55
speed of walking, 14, 46, 107
sprain prevention, 60
stair support (exercise), 97
steady state, 34
stomach muscles, 70
stress load, 92
stress reduction, 18, 58
stretching, 59–60, 68
sugars, 90

sun protection, 29
surface for walking, 30
take a bow (exercise), 62
tendons, bones, and ligaments, 59, 72
tension, 74, 83
testing the waters. See beginner's walking program
test results: A, 52, 80, 107; B or C, 52, 53, 79, 107; D, 53, 77, 107; E, 53, 107
thigh muscles, 62, 63, 64, 68, 69, 75
tiredness, 42
torso, 65
total body tension (exercise), 74
training heart rate, 37–39, 86
treadmill, 99–107; beginning, 107; features of, 103; and diagnosis, 101, 102; at home, 105–106; and walking test, 52, 107; for weight loss, 104
upper body, 45
vitamins, 89
walking in place (exercise), 97
walking program, choosing, 53. See also walking test
walking technique, 44–45
walking test, 46–53; length of, 47; for men, 48, 50, 52–53; for women, 49, 50, 52–53; and older people, 46; supplies for, 46; on treadmill, 52, 107
walking to work, 26
warm-up, 58–67; arm muscles, 66; calf muscles, 61; chest muscles, 65; exercises for, 61–67; helps movement and coordination, 60; for hip muscles, 63; neck muscles, 66; spine, 65; thighs, 62, 63, 64
water, how much to drink, 90
wave the flag (exercise), 65
weather, 26, 27, 93, 100
weight loss, 19, 21, 87–89, 104
weights, 31, 81
who should not walk, 20, 21, 22
who should walk, 13, 21
women: muscle mass, 50; and osteoporosis, 91; walking test evaluation, 49